Kobe Bryant: The Inspiring Story of One of Basketball's Greatest Shooting Guards

An Unauthorized Biography

By: Clayton Geoffreys

Visit my website at www.claytongeoffreys.com
Cover photo by Keith Allison is licensed under CC BY 2.0 / modified from original

Table of Contents

Foreword 1

Introduction 3

Chapter 1: Childhood and Early Life 7

Chapter 2: High School Years..12

Chapter 3: Kobe's NBA Career-The Early Years....................19

    Getting Drafted...19

    Rookie Season, Tough Times for the Young Teenager 32

    The Rise of the All-Star Teenage Kobe 39

Chapter 4: The Laker Dynasty 51

    The First of the Three-Peat...51

    The Second Title, Dominating the Playoffs 65

    Wrapping Up the Three-Peat...73

Chapter 5: Falling Out of the Kobe-Shaq Tandem 79

    The Beginning of the End of a Dynasty 79

    The Laker Super Team, the Final Days of the Los Angeles
Duo 89

The End of a Dynasty 95

Chapter 6: The Down Years.....................................99

First Season as a Lone Star in LA 99

First Scoring Title, the 81-Point Masterpiece....................101

Second Scoring Title, Losing to the Suns Again................109

Chapter 7: Bryant's Return to Glory.......................114

The MVP Season, Return Trip to the NBA Finals.............114

Fourth NBA Title, Return to the Top of the League 122

Fifth NBA Title 129

Chapter 8: Chasing MJ...136

The Fall From the Top..136

The Mamba Becoming Vino 139

Chapter 9: The Injury Years and Retirement 143

The Achilles Tear that Shattered a Career...........143

The Six-Game Season, the Fractured Knee.................147

Complete Body Breakdown, Kobe Trying to Defy Father Time..149

The Retirement Tour 151

Post-Retirement 153

Chapter 10: International Dominance 155

Chapter 11: Bryant's Personal Life........................162

Chapter 12: Impact on Basketball 169

Chapter 13: Kobe Bryant's Legacy and Future........173

Final Word/About the Author 177

References 180

Foreword

The Black Mamba. Few NBA players demand as much respect from players around the league as Kobe Bryant. Entering the NBA at the ripe age of eighteen, Kobe Bryant has become and remained a staple superstar in the NBA. It's no surprise why Kobe carries such high esteem with his name. Looking at his track record, Bryant retired a five-time NBA champion, two-time Finals MVP, eighteen-time All-Star and one-time MVP. Since entering the league, he defined Lakers basketball for the past two decades, including thrilling rides in the early 2000s with Shaquille O'Neal and later championship runs in the late 2000s. When people think of the words basketball genius, they think Kobe Bryant. Few players have ever brought as high of a level of intensity to the game of basketball as Bryant and few players have openly expressed their competitive drives as distinctly as Kobe. With the retirement of Kobe at the end of the 2015-2016 season, we can begin to process and reflect on the legendary career of the Black Mamba. Thank you for downloading *Kobe Bryant: The Inspiring Story of One of Basketball's Greatest Shooting Guards.* In this unauthorized biography, we will learn Kobe Bryant's incredible life story and impact on the game of basketball. Hope you enjoy and if you do, please do not forget to leave a review! Also, check out my website at claytongeoffreys.com to join my exclusive list where I let you know about my latest books and give you goodies!

Cheers,

Clayton Geoffreys

Visit me at www.claytongeoffreys.com

Introduction

When Lakers superstar Kobe Bryant gave himself the nickname Black Mamba, everyone wondered why he chose to liken himself to a reptile. The Black Mamba is one of the fastest and deadliest snakes in the world. It was also the codename used by Uma Thurman's assassin character in the Quentin Tarantino film *Kill Bill*. And yes, Black Mamba was also the boxing nickname given to Floyd Mayweather Jr.'s uncle, Roger Mayweather.

You may be thinking that Bryant definitely does not want to become a part of the Mayweather family, so it must have been that Tarantino movie that got to him. Well, it turns out that Bryant did, in fact, watch *Kill Bill* and was so intrigued by the codename Black Mamba that he did a bit of research on the snake. Upon reading up on the Mamba, Bryant decided that it was the perfect description of how he wanted his game to be.

The Black Mamba is said to have a 99% striking accuracy at high speeds and in rapid succession. Bryant stated that it is the kind of surgical precision that he wants in his game. Kobe Bryant has always been known as a perfectionist and player who, despite being great, still strives to be the greatest. And, like the Black Mamba, Kobe Bryant strikes with precision and without warning.

Bryant also talked about the Black Mamba mentality. He said that one has to, "figure it out, no matter what comes, whether it's hell or high water." This resilient attitude has been at the core of Bryant's game, and it is what has made him bounce back from the many obstacles he has faced on and off the court. In fact, this Mamba Mentality was what fueled him throughout his career as he challenged critics and supporters alike by continuing to work harder and harder to become the killer player that he has.

By using the Mamba Mentality that he made popular and staying true to his persona as the big black venomous snake, Kobe Bryant has chiseled his way to an NBA career worthy of being called one of the best of all time. He has nearly two decades of All-Stardom, five titles, an MVP award, and multiple memorable performances. Bryant has also become arguably one of the best of all time and is regarded as second only to Michael Jordan in his position, especially since him and the man known as the Greatest of All Time play and approach the game of basketball in an eerily similar fashion.

But while Michael Jordan carved his identity as the best player to have ever played using a combination of hard work, finesse, and methodological approach, Kobe Bryant's way of doing things was a lot different. He listened to all the critics and fueled himself with their words to push his body harder and harder to the point of breaking. Kobe was such a stubborn rebel of time and circumstance that not even injuries, age, or odds were able to keep him away from achieving his objectives. That was how he showed his passion for the game of basketball, which he regards as the mistress that nobody will ever love as much as he did.

With all his accomplishments and charisma, Kobe Bryant is one of the most famous basketball players on the planet. He is, without a doubt, one of the greatest scorers in the game and one of the most lethal offensive weapons to have ever graced the NBA's courts. However, Kobe Bryant is not all about scoring points. He is a winner, and he has proven that he can win on his own. Bryant is not just about basketball, either. He is also a million-dollar businessperson and worldwide icon. More importantly, Bryant is a husband, father, and son. Like all of us, he is only human and has committed many mistakes in his life. But unlike most of us, he is like a Black Mamba aiming for perfection and always striving for greatness.

It is that quest for greatness that has led Kobe Bryant to the NBA's basketball courts. It is that pursuit of greatness that has made him achieve what he has accomplished. And it's because of that quest for greatness that he still continues to play, even though he has reached the summit more than once.

What is that greatness all about, then?

Chapter 1: Childhood and Early Life

Kobe Bryant's greatness begins with his unique name. He was born with the name Kobe Bean Bryant to Joe and Pamela Bryant on August 23, 1978, in Philadelphia. He got his name from a steakhouse in the Philadelphia suburb of King of Prussia. Joe Bryant said he loved the name, so he called his first and only son Kobe, not knowing that he would one day outgrow the beef and the Japanese city from which it originates.

His middle name "Bean" is as compelling as his first name. His mother's maternal name was Pamela Cox, but his parents used the middle name "Bean" in honor of his father Joe, who was nicknamed "Jelly Bean" during his NBA days for his style of play. Joe was always bouncing around the court with very high energy.

Kobe Bryant is a second-generation NBA player. His father Joe played in the NBA after being selected by the Golden State Warriors as the 14th pick in the 1975 NBA draft. Joe Bryant's NBA career lasted for eight years, and he played for three NBA teams. Although he was drafted by the Warriors, he would debut as a member of the Philadelphia 76ers in the 1975-1976 season. He played 75 games where he averaged about 7.4 points per game. Although Joe Bryant played for four seasons with the

76ers, he had some of his best seasons playing with the San Diego Clippers. In the 1980-1981 season, he averaged 11.6 points per game with 5.4 rebounds and a shooting percentage of 47.9%. Those numbers went up when he started in more games in the 1981-1982 season where he averaged 11.8 points per game with a slightly higher 48.6% shooting percentage.

Joe Bryant ended his career in the NBA in 1983 when he last played for the Houston Rockets. He packed up his bags, brought along his family, and took his talents to Europe where he would become a star in the Italian League. In the Italian League, Joe played seven seasons with different clubs within the Italian A1 and A2 leagues. His first team was the AMG Sebastiani Rieti where he played for a couple of seasons. He then played with Viola Reggio Calabria for one year. After which, he transferred to Olimpia Pistoia where he played for two seasons, which was highlighted by his scoring 53 points in two games. Finally, he had two seasons with Reggio Emilia.

Life in Italy was great because Joe was a star, but five-year-old Kobe struggled because he did not know how to speak Italian. So together with his elder sisters, Shaya and Sharia, the Bryant siblings got together every day after school and helped each other learn the Italian language. Within a few months, they had learned how to speak Italian well and were able to communicate effectively with their peers.

After mastering the language, young Kobe set his sights on his father's sport – basketball. Even when he was three years old, and his father was still playing for the Clippers, Kobe Bryant already knew what he wanted to be when he grew up. When the Clippers game was on TV, he would put on his own Clippers jersey and mimic his father's moves the way he saw them on TV. He adored his father and wanted to be just like him.

Kobe learned to play basketball when he was in Italy. There, Bryant said the game was "all basic and no-nonsense," and learning the basics made him a very well-rounded basketball player. Although Kobe was getting better at basketball, it was not the number one sport in Italy.

Every time he showed up wanting to play basketball, kids asked him to participate in soccer matches. So Kobe honed his basketball skills by shooting hoops during the halftime breaks of his father's ballgames. Still, the influence of soccer got to him. As a kid, Kobe became a big fan of football heavyweight AC Milan and striker Marco Van Basten. Bryant even said that had he not pursued professional basketball, he would have wanted to be a soccer player. His length and athleticism made him an ideal goalkeeper, and as a kid, his playmates always let him play the role of goalie. Nevertheless, basketball was always his true love.

From the age of 10, Kobe and his family would return home to Philadelphia during the summer to visit family and friends and he would play in the Sonny Hill Summer League. Bryant struggled at first in that league, but his famous hard work ethic made him better and better as each year passed.

After some time, the Bryant family would move to France as Kobe's father played one season with FC Mulhouse Basket. Then, in the fall of 1991, his family would return to the United States for good. By then, Joe Bryant had played 16 professional basketball seasons. The family settled down in a comfortable home at the most prestigious suburban area in Philadelphia called Main Line. Joe Bryant was set to take on an unlikely career of coaching the girls' basketball team at a small school named Akiba Hebrew Academy in Lower Merion, Pennsylvania. Although Jellybean Bryant quit that coaching job in 1993 for an assistant coach position at his alma mater La Salle University, Lower Merion would become the most significant place of their lives.

Joe Bryant has coached many professional teams, and he still does until today. He started with the Las Vegas Rattlers of the

American Basketball Association, followed by the league's Boston Frenzy before spending one season with the Los Angeles Sparks after some time as an assistant. He would then coach a few teams in Japan and for the ASEAN Basketball League in Southeast Asia.

Chapter 2: High School Years

Thirteen-year-old Kobe Bryant enrolled at the Lower Merion High in Ardmore, Lower Merion. Similar to when he had moved to Italy as a kid, Bryant struggled to cope with the life at school because of the hip hop lifestyle of American teens. He said that it was strange at first because he did not even know a lot of the slang the kids were using. He just nodded as if he understood, but Bryant was later able to adapt to his new environment.

Basketball bridged the gap between his peers and himself. By then, he was a solid basketball player, and Bryant would become the first freshman to start for the Lower Merion varsity team. Despite the team finishing with a 4-20 record, a future star was born.

According to Gregg Downer, who was the head coach of the Lower Merion Aces at the time, he knew he had something special after watching Kobe Bryant play basketball for five minutes. Downer said he knew right then and there that Kobe would become a professional basketball player. He also believed that if he progressed smoothly and made the right decisions, he would get to the pros quickly. Downer was correct.

At age 14, Kobe Bryant vividly recalls the first time he tried to dunk the basketball. He said it was not much of a dunk because he barely grabbed the rim after the basketball went inside the hoop. It was a far cry from the spectacular dunks that he would soon throw down on bigger stages, but it pumped him up and encouraged him to become a better basketball player.

Kobe then blossomed into a high school superstar during his junior season, averaging 31.1 points, 10.4 rebounds, and 5.2 assists per game. Bryant won Pennsylvania Player of the Year honors that season and led the Aces to the state tournament with his incredible all-around skills. Bryant played point guard because he was an excellent playmaker. But aside from his passing abilities, Bryant led the team in scoring and rebounding. In a span of three seasons, Bryant had leaped to basketball stardom. But he was not yet contented with being the best high school basketball player in the nation.

During the summer before his senior season, Bryant worked out at the St. Joseph's University in Philadelphia where he played against better competition, including a handful of Philadelphia 76ers players and top college prospects. That summer turned out to be crucial. It was during this time that Bryant was receiving several offers from some great NCAA Division I men's basketball programs. Those programs included the Duke Blue

Devils, the Villanova Wildcats, the Michigan Wolverines, and even the North Carolina Tar Heels, where NBA legend Michael Jordan had played before becoming the league's star with the Chicago Bulls.

One of the first things he did in the summer before his senior year of high school was to participate in the Adidas ABCD basketball camp wherein he played alongside other NBA stars he would become very familiar with – including future teammate Lamar Odom. In that 1995 camp, Bryant would be given the Most Valuable Player award for all incoming senior student-athletes.

After a couple of weeks, Bryant would become a "regular" during the Sixers' practices at St. Joseph's Fieldhouse because the former 76ers head coach, John Lucas, would bring in top rookie prospects for the draft and use high school star Kobe Bryant as a measuring stick. By then, Bryant was one of a few talented high school players that were invited to be tested for their potential to play in the NBA.

Lucas remembers one day when Bryant stayed on the court after the practice to play one-on-one with the Sixers' rookie guard Jerry Stackhouse. Back in those days, Stackhouse was the 76ers franchise player and was one of the up-and-coming superstars of the NBA. 76ers assistant coach Tony DiLeo said that he did not know what the score was between Stackhouse and Bryant, but he was sure that Kobe "was doing very well" until coach Lucas ordered Stack and the high school kid to stop. It was not even important if Kobe won or lost against Jerry Stackhouse. Everyone who saw them play knew that Kobe was ready for the big league.

Kobe's dad also recalls one play during those scrimmages with the Sixers. His son was playing defense when suddenly, former Detroit Pistons Bad Boy Rick Mahorn set an NBA type of pick on a fragile Kobe Bryant. Mahorn floored him hard, but the resilient kid just jumped up and kept going. Joe Bryant said he knew then that his son was going to be very special.

Bryant would become the best high school player in the country during his senior season. He was more dominant than ever as he played all five positions on the court and averaged an astounding 30.8 points, 12 rebounds, 6.5 assists, four steals, and 3.8 blocks per game. He led the Aces to a 31-3 record and won for them their first State Championship in 53 seasons. The awards and accolades soon followed.

Bryant was named Naismith's High School Basketball Player of the Year, Gatorade Men's National Basketball Player of the

Year, and USA Today's National High School Player of the Year, among others. Bryant was also named to the McDonald's All-American All-Stars in addition to winning the 1995 Senior MVP award at the Adidas ABCD Camp. He ended his brilliant high school career as Pennsylvania's All-Time top scorer with 2,883 points, beating NBA greats Wilt Chamberlain and Lionel Simmons. In fact, his career scoring total was more than 500 points higher than what Chamberlain did during his years at Overbrook High School in Philadelphia, Pennsylvania in the early 1950s. Back then, Chamberlain went on to have a nice little NBA career of his own as a two-time champion and seven-time scoring champion. Likewise, Chamberlain was famous for scoring 100 points in a single game. Who knew it would not be the first time that Bryant's name was discussed in the same sentence as Chamberlain's when it came to scoring titles?

Bryant's success was not limited to the basketball court. He also scored big in his studies, scoring 1080 on his SAT, thereby ensuring that he could go to any college that he pleased. Top college programs like Duke, North Carolina, Villanova, and Michigan were the more prominent ones who knocked on his door, and although his parents wanted him to go to college, they knew that their son had a great shot at going directly to the pros.

In June of 1995, Farragut Academy High School star Kevin Garnett made the leap from high school to the NBA and was drafted by the Minnesota Timberwolves with the 5th pick in the 1995 NBA draft, becoming the first high schooler to do so since 1975. Garnett averaged 10.4 points, 6.8 rebounds and 1.8 assists per game during his rookie season where he was voted as part of the All-Rookie second team. But the transition was not easy, and Garnett did not immediately become an NBA star.

Faced with a tough decision to make, the Bryant family was at a crossroads. They believed that Kobe could duplicate KG's feat. However, that would involve throwing him into the lion's den, and there would be no turning back. There was also the concern about entering the real world without having gone to college first, which many star athletes pursue as a "plan B" in case they suffered a severe injury early in their professional career, or if things did not work out that well for them.

After weeks of soul searching and just before his prom night, Kobe Bryant held a news conference declaring that he would make himself available for the 1996 NBA draft. The news was met with mixed reviews. While some agreed that Kobe Bryant was ready, others criticized his parents for "pushing" their son into the big decision. The criticisms increased when Joe Bryant quit his assistant coaching job at La Salle to become his son's manager. The debate on whether Kobe would end up as a lottery pick like Kevin Garnett the year before officially began.

Chapter 3: Kobe's NBA Career-The Early Years

Getting Drafted

Before Bryant, there had only been five other prep-to-pro players, and Garnett was the fifth. The first was Reggie Harding, who was a fourth-round pick for the Detroit Pistons in 1962. He spent four seasons with the Pistons and the Bulls. Then there was Darryl Dawkins, who went to the 76ers in 1975 as the fifth overall selection. He became one of the most powerful slam dunk artists during that time. While in the NBA, he played for Philadelphia, New Jersey, Utah, and Detroit. He continued beyond the NBA with some teams in Italy and even had one year with the world-famous Harlem Globetrotters.

Then there was Bill Willoughby, who was a second-round pick from the same draft class as Dawkins. But he only averaged six points per game over eight seasons in the league with six different clubs. Finally, there was Garnett, who had an excellent rookie season with Minnesota. Thus, needless to say, Bryant had a lot of expectations to meet as he was entering the 1996 NBA Draft.

All five high school sensations were big men, either power forwards or centers whose basketball gifts were complemented with NBA size. On the other hand, Kobe was a lanky 6'6" who was considered a do-it-all guard. There were a lot of NBA guards who had his height and had the better physique, so Bryant was not a unique physical specimen at that time. Aside from physical attributes, there was something crucial that was not going Kobe's way heading into the draft.

There were many scouting reports being done by experts who were starting to come to his games during his senior year. One writer claimed to have difficulty to do so as Lower Merion High School held their boys' basketball games in front of thousands of loud fans, which possibly had an impact on his draft stock to the middle or later part of the first round. This problem was even reported by the folks at Upside Motor. It was originally published in the weeks leading up to the 1996 NBA Draft. Still, there were others who were able to find footage from that year's playoffs where he was able to show his ability to score and survey the defense for openings to shoot or pass the ball. Bryant was also noted for pushing the ball up court to keep opposing defenders on their heels. All of these highlighted his ability to do more than just score points. There were also several other scouting reports that pointed to Kobe Bryant's pedigree as a young high school star.

Physically, Bryant was as gifted as one can be. Standing nearly 6'6", Kobe was coming into the NBA as a forward with enough height and size for a then 17-year-old kid. On top of that, he was quick, athletic, and already strong for his age. Based on his physical attributes alone, Kobe Bryant was already a good enough prospect for a high school star making the jump to the NBA.

As what was often a trait lauded about him even when he was already winning championships as a youngster in the NBA, Kobe Bryant's maturity stood out back when he was still in high school.[i] Even at the tender age of 17, he was already as poised and mature as many other college basketball players. His maturity might have been a product of not only his pedigree as a second generation player, but also of his many travels as a young basketball phenom.

The maturity and well-roundedness also came from playing all five positions back in high school.[i] He was a point guard that could run the offense and see teammates well. He was a shooting guard with his ability to score the basket. He was a small forward that played the perimeter and the paint excellently on both ends of the floor. And he was a big man with the way he rebounded and scored inside baskets or at the post.

One other positive intangible attribute that Kobe Bryant already possessed coming into the NBA was his high basketball IQ and knowledge of the game of basketball.[i] Growing up, he was often a spectator of the many basketball stars that his father went up against in the NBA. And in many other countries, Kobe was instilled with the knowledge and the IQ that he might have been exposed to when Jellybean Bryant was off playing professional ball in international leagues. He has studied all of the greats back in the day and always did his homework, even until his twilight years as a professional player in 2016. Even as a young teenager, Bryant had always been the game's most diligent student.

Because of his size, athleticism, and well-roundedness in all aspects of the game, Kobe Bryant was projected to become the next coming of a then up-and-coming young superstar named Grant Hill.[i] Yes, at that age, Kobe was often compared to Grant Hill instead of Michael Jordan, who he now resembles more than any other legend. Bryant played a similar style as Hill did and was just as intelligent and versatile as the latter in his prime.

Despite the obvious pedigree and potential exuding from Kobe at such an early stage in his career, the soon-to-be NBA great had critics and weaknesses that turned several suitors off. Whether it was his age or inexperience, Kobe Bryant still had several detractors that thought he was not ready for the game.

A draft scouting report, which was the same one that described him as the next Grant Hill, said that Bryant did not have the ball handling skills nor the shooting ability to reach the level of stardom that Hill was at. He also did not have an exact position despite playing the small forward spot during the majority of his high school years since he was often playing every role at a good level, which was not high enough in the professional league. On top of all that, he was still a skinny teenager that might not have been ready for the life of an NBA player.[i]

NBA scouting director Marty Blake also once said that, "This kid can play" after watching Kobe Bryant in person. Nevertheless, for him, Bryant was still first and foremost a kid that he thought was not ready for the rigors of the NBA. In an interview with the LA Times in 1996, Blake even said that Bryant was kidding himself when the teenager stated that he wanted to come out of high school and straight into the NBA.[ii]

Then-Boston Celtics director for basketball development Jon Jennings also claimed that Kobe Bryant should never have entered the draft at that early point in his career. Comparing him to Garnett, Jennings said that KG was miles ahead of Kobe when the former tried his hand in the 1995 NBA Draft, but was nevertheless still not ready for the professional league. If Jennings thought Kevin Garnett was not ready for the NBA when he jumped straight out of high school, it was unadvisable for Kobe Bryant to follow his footsteps a year later.[ii]

Despite the many criticisms that Bryant faced coming into the NBA Draft, he would utterly destroy the words of his skeptics the moment he worked out for the teams that were interested in him. Bryant had worked out with the Los Angeles Lakers, the Phoenix Suns, the Boston Celtics, and the New Jersey Nets among others. All those teams' expectations and initial perception of Kobe Bryant were erased after the young 17-year old wowed them with his combination of skill and potential as a teenage phenom.

One notable workout that Kobe Bryant had was with the Boston Celtics, the Los Angeles Lakers' bitter rivals. ML Carr, who was the coach and executive vice president of the Celtics at that time, was thoroughly impressed with what Kobe Bryant did in both the workout and interview. Carr would say that Kobe was the best player he had ever interviewed, and the team's scouting director Rick Weitzman would say that Kobe could do everything.[iii]

Carr raved about Kobe Bryant to then Celtics president the late great Red Auerbach. He would recount how unbelievable Kobe's shooting exhibition was, especially the way his stroke looked so clean and beautiful. On top of that, the young Bryant had all the athleticism in the world with those young 17-year-old legs. He was so good during all the workouts that then-Celtics general manager John Volk immediately compared him to Michael Jordan, who was already a four-time NBA champion at that point in time.[iii]

What was even more impressive was Kobe's interview. Carr said that Kobe's knowledge about the game and the team's history was so advanced that he even knew more than any other Celtics player on the roster at that time. Bryant was indeed an excellent student of the game and was a one-of-a-kind talent that made Carr tell stories to Auerbach to convince him about the kid's skill level and potential.[iii]

Red Auerbach would give ML Carr the signal to draft whoever he wanted. Nevertheless, the Celtics, with the ninth pick in the draft tried to move up to sixth to get ahold of one of the six players that were regarded as better prospects. Those players were Allen Iverson, Marcus Camby, Ray Allen, Stephon Marbury, Antoine Walker, and Shareef Abdur-Rahim. Despite the awe of watching and listening to Kobe, the Boston Celtics were intent on drafting one of those six players.[iii] Hence, Kobe Bryant was not destined to become a Celtic.

Meanwhile, Kobe also went on to work out with several other teams that were in the running for a lottery pick. The Philadelphia 76ers, who had the luxury of the top overall pick, had Kobe Bryant running from baseline to baseline to see how fast he could go. The young Mamba was fast, really fast. But he was not fast enough to beat the time set by Allen Iverson, who was the favorite for the top spot because of how he obliterated the competition in college.

Bryant, who spent his high school years in Philadelphia as a phenom at Lower Merion High School, would have loved to play in Philly, where his father had also played back in his NBA days. However, when told by then-Sixers head coach Maurice Cheeks that Iverson was faster, Bryant was frustrated and was angered that how he did not understand what speed had to do with basketball.[iii]

One of the more legendary workouts that Bryant had before getting drafted was with the New Jersey Nets. Then-Nets head coach John Calipari was deeply interested in what Kobe could provide them. New Jersey had the eighth overall pick, especially after the Celtics moved their way up to the sixth spot. They would bring Kobe to Farleigh Dickinson University to see what the 17-year-old had to offer.

Kobe Bryant would go one-on-one with two decent Nets players at that time. One of those players was Ed O'Bannon, who was a decorated college basketball player back when Kobe was still in his early years as a high school player. O'Bannon, in his final year in college, was the NCAA Champion, the most outstanding player in the Final Four, and was awarded the prestigious John Wooden Award in his final year in 1995. He was the nation's best collegiate player during the 1994-95 season. However, Kobe Bryant destroyed O'Bannon in their workout.[iv]

The relentless attack that Kobe showed when pitted against O'Bannon prompted Calipari to declare that the young kid was better than anyone on the Nets roster at that time. Calipari was intent on drafting Kobe Bryant with the 8th pick. Nobody was going to stop him from doing so.

However, the Los Angeles Lakers had something to say about that. Kobe Bryant was also brought into Los Angeles to work out with some of the Lakers' players. Despite not even being in the position to draft a top prospect, the Lakers were looking to move up in the draft by trading away some of their key players as they looked for pieces to add to their roster in the hopes of signing Shaquille O'Neal to a lucrative deal.

Unlike the Nets, the Lakers did not just pit Kobe against a reliable NBA player. They had to put him one-on-one with one of the 80's Showtime Lakers legends Michael Cooper. Cooper, a member of several championship Lakers teams in the 80's, was not just some ordinary role player. He was the 1987 Defensive Player of the Year and had a lot of experience under his belt, especially since he was used to guarding Michael Jordan.

However, Kobe simply had no respect for the Laker legend as he destroyed him in their workout. Bryant was so good and competitive to the point that not even an established winner and legend in the NBA was enough to faze him. Kobe Bryant would even prompt Jerry West to declare him as the best player he had ever seen in a workout. West, like Calipari, would say that the 17-year-old kid was better than anyone on the Lakers' roster, which included the likes of borderline All-Stars Eddie Jones,

Nick Van Exel, and Cedric Ceballos.[ii] With Jerry West thoroughly impressed, he was intent on grabbing Kobe Bryant away from anyone who wished to pick him on draft day.

On draft day, the Philadelphia 76ers owned the top pick in the 1996 draft, and while coach John Lucas already saw Kobe Bryant at the St. Joseph scrimmages, the 1996 draft class was considered as one of the best, if not the best. Consequently, Kobe was not on top of Philadelphia's drafting list.

Ultimately, the 76ers chose Georgetown Hoya's Allen Iverson to become the first overall draft pick for that year. Iverson was a spitfire scoring guard who was destined to be one of the most influential players of this generation. The second pick went to the Toronto Raptors, who picked the shot-blocking demon Marcus Camby. Camby's defense was elite at the NBA level. Next were Sharif Abdur-Rahim, who was selected by the Vancouver Grizzlies, and Stephon Marbury, who went with the Minnesota Timberwolves. Both were one and done collegiate stars who had superstar potentials.

Then, there was Ray Allen, who was picked by the Milwaukee Bucks. Allen was a great clutch shooter who would later become the NBA's All-Time three-point leader. Other names included were Antoine Walker (Boston Celtics), Lorenzen

Wright (L.A. Clippers), Kerry Kittles (New Jersey Nets), Samaki Walker (Dallas Mavericks), Erick Dampier (Indiana Pacers), Todd Fuller (Golden State Warriors), and Vitaly Potapenko (Cleveland Cavaliers). These were some of the kids who had the collegiate experience that Kobe Bryant did not have. They had played at least one year in college where basketball was more organized, and the competition was better. But little did everyone know that Kobe Bryant was light years ahead of his rookie class in maturity and skill level. The kid was already a pro even before he was drafted.

When draft day came, twelve teams passed on Kobe Bryant before the Charlotte Hornets picked him. But the Hornets did not select him because they wanted him on their team. They picked him on the behest of Jerry West and the Los Angeles Lakers, who had made a prior deal to trade their Yugoslavian center Vlade Divac in exchange for the draft rights to Kobe Bryant. That deal raised a lot of eyebrows because Divac was one of the most popular players in Los Angeles and was developing into one of the better big men in the NBA. But Jerry West knew he had a diamond in the rough in Bryant, so he hatched a grand plan that would alter the destiny of the Lakers' franchise.

Despite concerns from fans who felt trading away their young and talented center could cause problems, West knew that the Lakers were going to sign free agent center Shaquille O'Neal that summer. Hence, Vlade Divac was deemed expendable in Lakers Land. He also knew that the Charlotte Hornets needed a big man, so he proposed a trade with the Hornets by offering Divac for their 13th pick. However, there was one more hitch.

The New Jersey Nets, who had worked out with Kobe three times, were also keen on selecting Kobe as the eighth pick after seeing what he did. This prompted West to pull a final trick from his sleeve. He talked Calipari out of drafting Bryant and encouraged Joe and Pam Bryant to tell Calipari that their son wanted to play for the Lakers. After all, it was public knowledge that Kobe was a huge fan of the Lakers and idolized Magic Johnson growing up.

On draft night, Calipari still tried to talk to Kobe and his agent, but they threatened to play in Italy if the Nets picked Bryant. The Nets ended up picking the more established Kerry Kittles while Kobe was picked by the Hornets and then traded to the Lakers to start one of the greatest legacies not only in the Lakers' franchise history but in the history of the NBA.

Rookie Season, Tough Times for the Young Teenager

After Kobe Bryant was drafted by the Los Angeles Lakers, the young kid, as a 17-year old still under parental guidance, needed his parents to co-sign his rookie contract to immediately become the youngest player to have ever signed an NBA contract. That record would not be broken for nearly a decade. It was not until 2005 when a younger Laker by the name of Andrew Bynum signed an NBA contract at a younger age than Kobe did.

As a rookie, Bryant was in a precarious situation coming into the NBA. Despite not joining a struggling team, he was set to play for one that had a lot of expectations on its shoulders because the Los Angeles Lakers have historically been the most successful and famous franchise in league history. Kobe was joining a team rearing to contend for a title as soon as the Lakers acquired Shaquille O'Neal in the offseason and were fielding good veteran players like Eddie Jones, Nick Van Exel, and Byron Scott. For a rookie, Kobe Bryant had a lot of expectations on his then slender shoulders as he was the draft pick that the Lakers had to sacrifice an established All-Star center on.

Kobe Bryant's NBA debut on November 3, 1996, was not an auspicious one. He went scoreless in six minutes of action in a game where he was just able to put up one field goal attempt against the Minnesota Timberwolves. Nevertheless, the Lakers still won 91-85 thanks to Shaquille O'Neal, who scored 35 points and collected 19 rebounds. But Bryant's struggles did not end on opening night.

Kobe would only score double digits in five of their first twenty games. He had 16 points against the Phoenix Suns on November 17, 1996, which became the highlight match. During that stretch of games, there were times when he only scored five points or less. In fact, there were many times when he scored nothing at all. In these games, he came mostly from the bench and only played about five to eight minutes at a time. This was even though he was considered to be the next heir to the throne that was once held by Michael Jordan, who was entering his final seasons en route to another three-peat of the NBA Championship with the Chicago Bulls.

Speaking of Jordan, the 1996 season showed the first time Bryant and Jordan dressed up against each other. On December 17, 1996, Bryant was still a reserve player coming off the bench and only scored five points in 10 minutes. On the other side of the court, Jordan had 30 points, nine rebounds, three assists, a steal, and a block as the Bulls defeated the Lakers 129-123. Technically, this was the first round of what fans would continue to debate on for years – it just did not seem like it at the time.

Kobe's struggles were partly because he played limited minutes since Nick Van Exel and Eddie Jones were eating up the minutes at the guard position. However, as the season progressed, so did Kobe's minutes. He began to be known for his high-flying acts and dazzling moves on the court. He surpassed the 20-point mark on January 3, 1997, when the Lakers defeated the Sacramento Kings 100-93. He got 6 out of 10 from the field and 9 out of 10 free throws for 21 points. The only player to score more points in the game was Elden Campbell, who had 22 points and 15 rebounds.

It was fitting that Kobe got the invitation to participate in the 1997 Slam Dunk competition at Cleveland's Gund Arena in February. After a slow start in the first round, Bryant mesmerized the crowd with a between-the-legs dunk to win the contest. In doing so, Bryant did not only become the NBA's newest Slam Dunk King, he became the youngest player to win the All-Star Break dunk contest at 18 years of age.

In addition to his slam dunk performance, Bryant also contributed in the league's fourth annual NBA Rookie Challenge Game where the first-year players in the Western Conference fell to the Eastern Conference 96-91. However, Bryant bested all scoring players with 31 points, eight rebounds, three assists, two steals, and one blocked shot.

Kobe's victory in the Slam Dunk contest proved to be the crowning glory of his rookie season. His minutes were slowly increasing together with his average points per game because he had more chances to score. He scored more than 20 points a few more times in the season, but did not get any double-doubles throughout the season. The longest he ever played was on March 27, 1997, when the Lakers were able to get a close overtime win on the road over the Vancouver Grizzlies, 102-98. Bryant played a total of 43 minutes on the court in one of his earliest known starts and had 20 points, eight rebounds, four assists, and three steals.

The Lakers ended the season with 56 wins, which was just enough to get them the fourth place slot in the Western Conference. The Lakers bested the Blazers 3-1 in the first round of the playoffs. In each of the Lakers' three wins, Bryant scored two, six, and zero points respectively with six or fewer minutes of time on the court in each game. Although Bryant did have 27 minutes of playing time in Game 3 in Portland where he scored 22 points, of which two of three were from behind the three-point line off the bench, the Lakers would lose that game 98-90. However, they were still able to win the series and move on to the conference semifinals against the top-seeded Utah Jazz.

The Jazz utilized their home court advantage to win the first two games at home, with Bryant only playing a total of eight minutes in both games. But the Lakers crawled back in Game 3 at the Staples Center on May 8, 1997, where Kobe scored 19 points off the bench. Thirteen of Bryant's points came from the foul line where he missed just one attempt. However, that win turned out to be the Lakers' last hurrah as the Jazz took a commanding 3-1 lead by winning Game 4 on May 10, 1997, where Bryant would score only nine points for 28 minutes on the court. Only three of his nine field goal attempts went in.

Bryant's rookie season came to an end in Game 5 of the Western Conference Semifinals against the Jazz where he shot those four infamous air balls. Kobe Bryant shot 4 out of 14 from the field and missed all six of his attempts from the three-point distance and finished the game with just 11 points. He even air-balled the one that would have tied the game and send it to an extra period. The Lakers would lose that game 98-93. As the Lakers' duo walked off the court, Shaquille O' Neal told a dejected Kobe Bryant to "go home, work hard, and come back next year." Bryant took that to heart, and he returned a better player the following season.

However, nobody could fault or blame the Lakers' young guard for attempting or shooting those air balls. Kobe, as a teenager, was the only one willing to try to bail out his team in those kinds of situations, even though he was the youngest member of the squad. Back then, he already showed supreme confidence in his skills even as the Laker fans and the whole world were making him a laughing stock. Nothing could deter Kobe Bryant's confidence.

"People around me, meaning the media and coaching staff, really looked at those shots as kind of being a turning point. I just basically looked at it as giving me more confidence. Even though I didn't hit the shots, I knew that my teammates had confidence in me to take the shots," said Kobe in an interview with the Los Angeles Times back in 1997.

Little did everyone know that those air balls were what transformed Kobe Bryant into the international basketball sensation he is today. Bryant would use those missed shots to fuel his desires of becoming the best player he could possibly be. "It was an early turning point for me in being able to deal with adversity," said Kobe Bryant when he recalled the air balls when he was still 18.[v]

In 2015, Bryant's former teammate and then head coach Byron Scott would remember how Kobe was both brave enough to take those shots and mature enough to grow from those misses and become one of the greatest of all time.[ii] At only 18 years old, Bryant already showed the confidence and fearlessness to take the shots nobody wanted to and to absorb all the ridicule and criticism that no other players were willing to take.

Not to put himself down for every criticism he faced because of those air balls, Kobe Bryant would work on his shot alone every single day until sunrise. He would endlessly shoot jumper after jumper to rectify one of his weaknesses early on in his career. It would not take long until Kobe's jumpers would become the deadliest weapon the league had seen in his era.[v]

After averaging 7.6 points on 41.7% shooting in only 15 minutes of action in his rookie year, Kobe Bryant still had many believers, particularly in the Laker organization. Cedric Ceballos would call Bryant a talented individual, not only regarding skills, but also in the way he mentally focused on basketball. It was a trait not a lot of players had in the history of the league.[ii]

Then-head coach Dell Harris even remembered how supremely confident Bryant was, even at 18 years old, to the point that he may have even seemed cocky. Harris recalled how Kobe would often ask his coach just to give him the ball and have everyone clear out of his way because he believed himself to be able to beat any defender, whether it was from the perimeter or down at the low post. But Harris, as he remembered, did not give Kobe Bryant the free reigns to do so, especially when Shaquille O'Neal was patrolling the paint.[ii]

The Rise of the All-Star Teenage Kobe

Despite a lackluster rookie season for the teenage phenom, all the hard work fueled by criticism and ridicule paid off for the soon-to-be Black Mamba of the NBA. In his second season, Kobe Bryant would show more flashes of his future superstar self. Comparisons to a younger version of Michael Jordan only surfaced more and more as the young teenage star's talents only became more apparent.

At one point, his teammate Robert Horry even claimed that Kobe Bryant, with all his skills and abilities as a young teenager, had what it took to become the game's all-time leading scorer. Even Shaquille O'Neal would say that Kobe was the future of the NBA. While not entirely correct in their statements, neither

Horry nor O'Neal were wrong about the apparent talent and potential within the young Bryant.

In the first game of his sophomore season, Bryant would score 23 points in 33 minutes off the bench in the team's 104-87 win over the defending Western Conference Champions on October 31, 1997. This game was a little bit of revenge for Los Angeles after being eliminated from the playoffs the year before. There were still some shooting struggles as Bryant only made about 38.5 percent of his shots in that game. He struggled more in the next with a field goal percentage of 20 in the next game held on November 4, 1997. Bryant only had one field goal and a few free throws to get four points in the Lakers' 99-94 win over the New York Knicks. The Lakers were rolling after winning their first eight games of the season.

After two games of lackluster performances, Kobe Bryant would become a centerpiece of a 35-point demolition job over the Golden State Warriors in his fourth game that season. In only 24 minutes of action, he hit 11 field goal attempts to score 25 points. The rampage would continue as Kobe Bryant would score in double digits for seven more consecutive games after that performance.

For the first time in his young career, Kobe Bryant would break the 30-point mark when he scored 30 points in a blowout win over the Dallas Mavericks on December 14, 1998. In only 32 minutes of action, he was 12 out of 21 from the field. That game was after he recorded a then-season high of 27 points in a win over the Houston Rockets.

Then, in what was his first chance to show Michael Jordan his new moves and improved skills, Kobe Bryant and his Los Angeles Lakers marched into Chicago on December 17 for a matchup between the established greatest player and the younger heir apparent. Despite a loss on the part of the Lakers, Bryant and Jordan seemed like they were playing a game within a game as they tried to outmatch each other during every single play.

In the end, it was MJ who won out by scoring 36 points. He also had five rebounds and four assists to make sure that a younger, fresher player could not steal his throne and spotlight. Kobe was not too shabby either with 33 points on 12 out of 20 shooting from the field off the bench. He also made 3 of his five three-pointers as he proved that he was no longer the rookie that air balled all those outside attempts. Those 33 points were the best he mustered up all season long as he faced the best player in all of basketball.

As the season progressed, Bryant continued to improve despite having games where he would see the court briefly and other games where he would see plenty of action. The most minutes he saw in a competition was an overtime loss to the Seattle SuperSonics on February 13, 1998, where Bryant was 4 out of 13 and made all seven free throws for 15 points in the game.

Bryant doubled his scoring average in his sophomore season to 15.6 points per game as his playing time increased to 26.0 minutes per game. Despite his improvement, Bryant started only one game that season. But that did not stop the fans from voting for the popular teenager as a starter for the Western Conference All-Star team.

As Bryant joined teammates Shaquille O'Neal, Nick Van Exel, and Edie Jones in the Western Conference squad, Bryant became the youngest player in the history of the NBA to start in an All-Star team. On February 8, 1998, at Madison Square Garden in New York City, Bryant would score 18 points after shooting 7 out of 16 from the field with six rebounds, two steals, and one assist. He led everyone on his Western Conference team, but they would lose to the East, 135-114. The East was led by Jordan once again, who scored 23 points, eight assists, and six rebounds. Granted that team also included Shawn Kemp, Grant Hill, Dikembe Mutombo, and Reggie Miller.

However, what was the highlight of that All-Star game was the game within the game between Kobe Bryant and Michael Jordan. Kobe was the challenger while Mike was the unchallenged king. Even at the tender age of 19, Bryant was not afraid to stare into the eyes of the most legendary player the world has ever seen. Kobe relentlessly attacked the GOAT without an ounce of fear while putting on a show for the crowd with highlight dunks and moves, which even included an impossible-looking skyhook as he was running out of bounds. At one point, he even waved off Karl Malone's screen (to his irritation) so that he could go one-on-one with the great one.[vi]

On the part of Michael Jordan, the undisputed legend saw a glimpse of his younger self in Kobe Bryant. The attacking mentality, the fearless challenge, the ability to sense weakness (Jordan was already old and hobbling at that time), and the unwavering competitive nature were all attributes that Jordan once had and admired in the young Bryant. Mike would say that, if he were in the very same position as Kobe was, he would have done the same things that the young star did to him.[vi] And even as MJ walked out the victory in that matchup, nobody could discount the historical show that Kobe put up that night.

As the leading scorer for the Lakers' second unit, Bryant finished second in the voting for the NBA's Sixth Man of the

Year award, which went to Danny Manning of the Phoenix Suns. The Lakers finished the season 61-21 and second place in the Pacific Division behind Seattle, and would finish with the third seed in the Western Conference playoffs

The 1998 playoffs were a mixed bag of good and bad games for Bryant. In the first game of the best-of-five first-round series of the Western Conference playoffs, Bryant scored 15 points on 44.4 percent field goal shooting in a 104-102 win over the Portland Trail Blazers on April 24, 1998. In nearly the same amount of time, he only scored four points each in both Games 2 and 3 – which Los Angeles split before they took the series in Game 4 on April 30, 1998, in Portland's Rose Garden. Bryant played much better in that game with 22 points, shooting about 56.3 percent from the field (nine out of 16) while collecting three rebounds on defense, one block, and four assists.

Los Angeles would take care of their Pacific Division rivals from Seattle in just five games in what was scheduled to be a best-of-seven in the conference semifinals. Bryant was limited in action, scoring less than five points in most of the games.

However, he was back to being a contributor with 16 points in the Game 1 loss to the Utah Jazz on May 16, 1998, at 112-77. But Bryant's numbers would continue to decrease as he would end up shooting about 40.8 percent from the field, about 21 percent from beyond the three-point line, and just under 70 percent from the free-throw line for all four games in the Western Conference Finals. Utah would win again and move on to face the Bulls in what would be Jordan's sixth and final NBA Championship in the NBA.

Michael Jordan went on to retire at the end of that season after winning his sixth and final NBA championship, and Kobe Bryant's rise to stardom only made the comparisons between the two players a regular topic of conversation. There was no question what an impact Mike had on the game since he came into the league in 1984. However, nobody in the history of the NBA had absorbed all of Jordan's influence more than Kobe Bryant.

His teammate Jon Barry once said that Kobe could do everything that Mike could do and that he was not even sure if Jordan could even do some of the things that Bryant could. And for Kobe's part, he was not even bothered by the comparisons because, after all, he had all the confidence in the world to believe and expect that he would be just as good, or even better than Jordan was at his prime.[ii]

Nobody could be blamed for trying to compare Kobe Bryant to Michael Jordan. They play the same positions. They are just about the same size. They were both excellent athletes at the height of their physical abilities. Skill wise, Bryant had the same set of skills that Jordan had. However, the mental side of the game was where they were both eerily similar. Kobe was just as competitive, focused, and determined as Mike was. On top of all those, both players possessed the charisma and abilities to put on a show every time they were on the floor.

Speaking of putting on a show, that was a part of Kobe Bryant's game that often got him criticized. "Showboat" was a nickname he was often called back in the day because of his penchant for putting up highlight reel plays every time he had the ball in his hands. Instead of making the right plays at the right moments, Kobe would often attempt the most spectacular shot, dribble, or dunk he could find in his bag of tricks, sometimes to the detriment of the team and flow of the game.

Kobe Bryant's showboating ways did not always entertain the people that mattered most—his teammates and coaches. Assistant coach Kurt Rambis once had an argument with Bryant in a game because the latter would often disrupt the flow of the game so that he could put on a show. "Fine, do whatever what you want to do," said Rambis. Jerry West, the general manager, even told Bryant that he should never associate himself with the word "Showboat" if he wanted to be associated with greatness. And as Bryant's accomplishments would show later in his prime years, the Laker star responded to what West challenged him to do.

A labor dispute fueled the lockout that shortened the 1999 NBA season. Nevertheless, it became Kobe's breakout year. With Nick Van Exel and Eddie Jones gone via trade, Bryant became the new focal point of the backcourt and a leading contributor in the offense.

As Kobe's talents, confidence, and maturity grew, the whole league and Laker coaches began to trust him with the offense more and more. He and Shaq were destined to become the greatest one-two punch and inside-outside duo the NBA has ever seen. Bryant's playing time increased to 37.9 minutes per game, and he responded by averaging a shade below 20 points per game while also averaging 5.3 points, 3.8 assists, and 1.4 steals. Aside from getting the bulk of the minutes at shooting guard, Bryant started all 50 games during the regular season.

In the first game of the season on February 5, 1999, Bryant had his first double-double with 25 points and ten rebounds in a win over the Houston Rockets. In fact, Bryant had started his third season in the league with five double-doubles thanks to a shooting percentage of about 44.3 during the run. It was also a display of his supreme athleticism and tenacity for the ball. Kobe was chasing possession after possession while scoring the ball just as well when he got it up to the attack zone.

Kobe was also very close to his first triple-double on February 22, 1999, in an overtime loss to the Denver Nuggets (117-113). Bryant scored 26 points on 53.3 percent from the field and 9 out of 11 from the free-throw line while collecting 13 rebounds – 12 while playing defense – and nine assists. More went to teammate Shaquille O'Neal who led the team with 28 points and seven rebounds. This duo was starting to show signs of life as a good combination of power, speed, rebounding, and shooting.

Kobe Bryant would break the 30-point mark for the first time that season when he had 32 points on 11 out of 19 shooting from the field against the Phoenix Suns in another win for the Lakers, who would go on to win ten straight games during that juncture. Bryant would only score below 10 points in two of those games and started to see a lot of consistency on both ends of the floor.

Bryant almost hit the 40-point mark with 38 points in a win while visiting the Orlando Magic (115-104) on March 21, 1999. He made 15 of 24 shots from the field (62.5 percent) while collecting four assists, three rebounds, two steals, and a block. O'Neal also added 31 points with 13 rebounds of his own in that game.

It was an improved season as Bryant started in all but one game of the shortened season. The Lakers finished with a record of 31-19 and second in the Pacific Division behind the Portland Trail Blazers and the fourth seed in the 1999 Western Conference Playoffs. That meant they were put against the Houston Rockets and were able to sneak a 101-100 win in the first game of a best-of-five first-round series where Bryant scored 17 points and five rebounds on May 9, 1999.

Bryant would follow that up with a double-double in Game 2 with 19 points and nine rebounds to support O'Neal's 28 points and nine rebounds for a 110-98 win at home on May 11, 1999. The Rockets would get one win in Game 3 at 102-88, but would drop the fourth game and the series on May 15, 1999, when the Lakers defeated the Rockets 98-88. While O'Neal was the star with 37 points and 11 rebounds, Bryant had 24 points and eight assists despite making 9 out of 25 shot attempts (36.0 percent).

But the postseason was no different from the previous year, and the Lakers were swept by the San Antonio Spurs 4-0 in the conference semifinals. The Spurs featured a young Tim Duncan and the veteran David Robinson under head coach Gregg Popovich. This team would begin their dynasty to start the new era of the NBA without the dominant Chicago Bulls composed of Jordan, Scottie Pippen, and Dennis Rodman. Bryant would have some good games with 21 points on 47.1 percent shooting from the field on May 17, 1999, and another 28 points in Game 2 about four days later where he would make 12 of 25 field goals (48.0 percent) with eight rebounds and four assists. But his ability to score would drop off with only 20 and 16 points respectively in Games 3 and 4 as the Spurs would move on and defeat the New York Knicks in five games during the 1999 NBA Finals.

It was a great run for the Lakers, who had three different coaches after letting Del Harris leave the team after a 6-6 start to the season. Bill Bertka took over for one game as an interim replacement before the Lakers brought in Kurt Rambis, who was 24-13 during his short term with the Lakers. Sometimes, opportunities can knock at the right time and begin a new era with a well-known coach to help a young star like Bryant flourish.

Chapter 4: The Laker Dynasty

The First of the Three-Peat

The 2000 season became the first major turning point in Kobe Bryant's career. After three different coaches the previous season, the Lakers settled down with former Chicago Bulls Head Coach Phil Jackson. Jackson had retired after the Bulls won the last of their 6 NBA titles in 1998. The Bulls had two three-peat championship runs from 1991 to 1993, and again from 1996 to 1998. Jackson claimed that he would never coach again, but the lure of a talented team in Los Angeles was too much to say no to.

The hiring of Phil Jackson only led to more Bryant-Jordan comparisons. It was the "Zen Master" who was responsible for implementing the system that helped Mike win six NBA championships and several other MVP awards. While Bryant was already showing flashes of a young Jordan as early as his third season, one could only speculate how much more Jordanesque he could become, especially with Phil Jackson on board.

Jackson brought along with him Tex Winters, the godfather of the triangle offense, which worked like magic in Chicago.

Together, they instilled the system in Los Angeles, and it immediately reaped wonders for the rising star Kobe Bryant. Bryant thrived in Jackson's triangle system as Michael Jordan had in Chicago. The keys to the triangle system are spacing and movement. But in case the defense shuts it down during the latter part of the shot clock, the bailout play is an isolation play where scorers like MJ and Kobe are at their best. The spacing that happens in a triangle offense gives great isolation scorers like Kobe Bryant enough space to operate and score at higher rates. In the triangle offense, there are no set positions. Hence, guards like Kobe, who are excellent post scorers, benefit from the system.

Despite the fact that Kobe Bryant was set to play in a system he never played under before, the triangle offense was not foreign to him. Even before he knew that Jackson and Winters were going to coach the Lakers, Bryant admitted to calling Tex back that day to ask him about the mysterious offense that helped Jordan and the Bulls win six titles. He talked with Winters for an hour until he understood what the triangle was all about.[vii]

However, under the Laker's triangle, Kobe Bryant was not the focal point, unlike when Michael Jordan played that role in his days with the Bulls. The focus of their triangle was Shaquille O'Neal, who is arguably the most dominant post presence in the history of the NBA. Nevertheless, Kobe still thrived as the second key piece of the triangle offense since O'Neal needed to regularly kick passes out or find cutters whenever he was not available for a basket. Bryant played that role perfectly.

After a few games of getting used to the new system helped him break the 20-point scoring average mark for the season – the first time in his career – he posted an average of 22.5 points per game on top of 6.3 rebounds and 4.9 assists per game. Bryant also had the best true shooting percentage and effective field goal percentage of his young four-year career.

Despite all the positivity surrounding the Lakers, who were quite sure of their dominance that season, Bryant would miss the first 15 games of the season due to a wrist injury before the opening week. He would make his return on December 1, 1999, when he was coming off the bench for the first four games.

Kobe Bryant would start the season on a high note as his scoring ways coupled with Shaquille O'Neal's dominance down low paved the way for a 4-0 start while he was playing for the Los Angeles Lakers. While Bryant was still struggling to adjust to the nuances of the triangle offense, he still found himself scoring well in the early stages of the season, especially because of how relentlessly he attacked the basket.

Fully healed and committed to a championship run for the Lakers, Kobe Bryant would score 30 for the first time that season as he attacked the Atlanta Hawks both from the perimeter and foul stripe. One day later on December 17, he scored 28 points and dished out 12 assists to display a side of him rarely seen. Under a system that involved a lot of ball movement, Kobe Bryant started to pass the ball more, and the Lakers rolled to a 20-1 start in the first 21 games since the star shooting guard's return from injury. In two of those wins, Bryant even scored back-to-back 30-point games for the first time in his career and was shooting a total of 23 out of 36 from the field.

With the way Kobe was playing that season, the Laker star would see his second All-Star appearance after the midseason classic skipped a year due to the lockout. While it was his teammate Shaquille O'Neal who won the All-Star MVP award together with Tim Duncan, Bryant did well in his second All-Star game, scoring 15 points as a starter for the Western Conference squad.

As soon as the season resumed, Kobe Bryant and the Lakers continued their relentless assault over the rest of the league. The team was unbeatable on their way to 19 consecutive victories in a span of nearly two months.

One of Bryant's best games in that winning streak was on March 12, 2000, when they defeated the Sacramento Kings, 109-106. Bryant scored 40 points – the first time he had hit that mark in his career. He shot 15 of 24 from the field (62.5 percent) and made eight of his nine free throws. Additionally, he collected ten rebounds and eight assists for a near triple-double. Bryant was starting to become a much more capable shooter with games where he rarely missed. The team was also supported by their big man at center, Shaquille O'Neal, with 39 points and 20 rebounds.

On March 6, 2000, Bryant was 9 of 12 from the field for a 75 field goal percentage for 22 points in the Lakers' 123-103 win over inner-city rivals, the Clippers. This came about a week after shooting 72.2 percent from the field (13 out of 18) for 31 points in another wide-margined victory over the Houston Rockets, 101-85. And while he was showing improved defense, Bryant would start to show signs of being a key defender.

Bryant earned a spot on the NBA's All-Defensive First Team unit in 2000, which he would be awarded eight more times (2003-2004, 2006-2011). He was the youngest to become part of that squad as he was also a member of the All-NBA Second Team. One of his strongest defensive games was when he collected five steals in an 88-78 win at the United Center in

55

Chicago over the Bulls on February 15, 2000. There were also two games where Bryant would block five shots in each – December 11, 1999, against the Vancouver Grizzlies (106-94), and on February 20, 2000, against the Philadelphia 76ers (87-84).

The Lakers romped to a 67-15 regular season record, the fifth-best in NBA history, and the Lakers' best record since the magical 69-win season of 1971-72. It was a culmination of what was a great one-two punch duo of Kobe Bryant and Shaquille O'Neal, who both proved their dominance at their respective places on the floor. Phil Jackson's triangle offense also proved invaluable, and Bryant thrived in the system.

In the opening round of the Western Conference playoffs, the Lakers were able to top the Sacramento Kings, winning the series 3-2. Bryant had three games where he scored more than 30 points, including 35 points on April 30, 2000. In fact, Bryant was on fire from the field, shooting 49.6 percent and averaging nearly four assists and just over one steal per game. However, the series was not an easy one for the Lakers. The Kings were growing to become their biggest rivals in that era of basketball.

After soundly beating Sacramento in the Games 1 and 2 with a combined difference of 34 points, the Lakers found themselves at a roadblock when the series shifted to the home of the Kings. As the Lakers methodically used their triangle offense in the first two games of the series while focusing the offense on the dominant duo of Kobe and Shaq, Sacramento would tighten the paint to frustrate the Big Diesel in Games 3 and 4. Meanwhile, they would gamble on Kobe to do the damage, and he averaged 33.5 points in those two games in Sacramento. But as soon as the series returned to Los Angeles for a pivotal Game 5, O'Neal dominated the paint to win the first round.

Bryant and the Lakers continued the momentum by defeating the Phoenix Suns 4-1 in the Western Conference Semifinals. He averaged 21 points per game despite shooting only 15.4 percent from behind the arc. Most of the Laker offense was centered on O'Neal, who was averaging a little more than 30 points per game with 16.2 rebounds per game and making about 55.9 percent of his total shots inside the paint.

The Suns were fielding a good defensive backcourt duo of Jason Kidd and Penny Hardaway. Their primary focus was stopping Kobe Bryant from scoring, and the Laker backcourt star struggled to get up a shot in all five games of the series. However, nobody on the Sun's roster was big or strong enough stop Shaq from dominating as Superman lorded over Phoenix for an easy five-game series win.

The Lakers raced to the conference finals, but found themselves in a dogfight against an equally-talented Portland Trail Blazers. If Kobe already found the Phoenix backcourt a formidable defensive duo to contend with, the Portland Trail Blazers' perimeter defense was even tougher. Shooting guard Steve Smith was a decent defender, but it was Scottie Pippen who frustrated Kobe the most.

Scottie Pippen, a few years fresh from his three-peat as a Chicago Bull, has always been regarded as one of the best perimeter defenders in league history. While he had already slowed down with age when they battled the Lakers in the Conference Finals, his experience as a student of Phil Jackson and a teammate of Michael Jordan helped him defend Kobe with sheer excellence.

In Game 1 of that series, Bryant could not even get up a shot as Portland's defense denied him of possessions and good open looks. However, it was Shaquille O'Neal to the rescue again. The newly crowned league MVP scored 41 big points to win the game for the Lakers. Game 2 was more of the same for Kobe as he combined for a total of 6 out of 18 shooting from the field in the first two games of the series. Moreover, the Blazers found a way to stop Shaq to tie the series 1-1.

In what was a relieving game for Kobe, Game 3 saw Bryant and O'Neal scoring well for the first time in that series as the duo combined for 51 points against the same tough defense that had covered them well in three games. The Lakers would win Game 3 by a slim margin of two points. While Game 3 was another tough shooting night for Kobe, the Lakers won it thanks to the production of former All-Stars Ron Harper and Glen Rice, who both provided good veteran leadership and experience all season long. With that win, Los Angeles was up 3-1 and was looking to close the series out.

However, the Blazers had other plans, and continued to cover the perimeter well to force Kobe Bryant to struggle yet again. Despite allowing Shaq to score 31 points and grab 21 rebounds in Game 5, the Blazers knew that the Lakers needed Bryant to contribute as they won the game methodically on the defensive end. And since both Bryant and O'Neal played all 48 minutes of Game 6, the Portland Trail Blazers would now focus their attention on the Big Aristotle, who struggled with his shot. Despite the breakout 33 points from Kobe, Portland won the bout and tied the series 3-3.

Playing in Los Angeles for all the marbles, the Blazers summoned all their energy to take a 13-point lead at the start of the fourth quarter of Game 7. Shaq was once again struggling to get possession of the ball. Meanwhile, it was Bryant who saved the day for the Los Angeles Lakers with one of his most famous clutch performance. The young superstar fueled a miraculous rally in the final 12 minutes as the Lakers finished the game with a scintillating run capped by Kobe Bryant's great alley-oop pass to an awed Shaquille O'Neal, which gave the Lakers the lead for good. The alley-oop remains one of the most memorable moments in NBA playoff history. Bryant finished the game with 25 points, 11 rebounds, seven assists, and four blocks in a career-defining performance for both Kobe and Shaq.

Having conquered their biggest challenge of the season, the Lakers were on their way to the Finals in their first appearance on the grandest stage since the days of Magic Johnson and James Worthy. Standing in the way of their return to the pinnacle of the NBA were the Indiana Pacers, who were running on Reggie Miller's hunger for exorcising the Jordan demons that had prevented him from breaking out of the East in the 90's. However, he was about to meet a player in the same mold as Michael Jordan in the form of Kobe Bryant.

Game 1 of the series was a no-contest for the Lakers. Shaquille O'Neal dominated the paint for another huge scoring night. Meanwhile, Kobe, who only had 14 points, did just enough to attract defenders on his side while his teammate lorded over smaller defenders in the paint. With that win, things looked easy for the Lakers, who were hungry for a title to add to their already remarkable collection of trophies.

However, Game 2 turned out to be one of the toughest moments for Kobe Bryant and the Los Angeles Lakers. The Pacers assigned a good defender in the form of Jalen Rose to cover Kobe Bryant. As Bryant attempted a jumper early in the second quarter, Rose went out to contest him. While the defense worked since Kobe missed the shot, the aftermath was even worse, and he landed on Rose's foot. Hobbled and injured, Kobe Bryant left the game in only 9 minutes of action. He would even miss the next match. But the Lakers won that game even without him.

Fast forward 12 years later to one of ESPN's segments. Jalen Rose recounted how he should have earned a ring had Kobe Bryant missed the whole series. That was how important he thought Kobe was to the Lakers. But when asked if he intentionally tried to take Bryant out, Rose would admit that he probably did it on purpose in the heat of the moment of trying to win a title. Nevertheless, Bryant would survive the assault on his body and would come back for Game 4 after the Pacers won Game 3.

Kobe Bryant's return in Game 4 was the pivotal moment of the series. While Shaquille O'Neal was the runaway most dominant player of that series, the Lakers might not have won the title if it were not for Bryant's clutch Game 4 performance. He would score 22 points in only the second half as O'Neal fouled out of the match, frustrated with the defense he was seeing. Without Shaq in the overtime period, it was up to Kobe to save the day as he hit the game-winning shot that put the Lakers up for good at 3-1 in the series.

A clutch player himself, Derek Fisher was just as awed and impressed by Kobe's Game 4 performance as anybody else. He would compare Bryant to the legendary Lakers of old. Fisher watched Magic Johnson and Kareem Abdul-Jabbar taking over important playoff games during their best years. He ranked Kobe Bryant's performance up there with the best that Magic and Kareem could muster.[ii]

Even opposing players were made believers by what Kobe did in Game 4. The Pacers' Sam Perkins, a veteran of the old NBA ruled by Michael Jordan, compared Kobe's competitiveness to the same level as MJ's. Perkins remarked how much Kobe Bryant had progressed from that kid that tried to win the game with those air balls in Utah to the superstar he was in 2000, especially with the performance he put up in Game 4 of the Finals.[ii]

In what was his worst performance of the Finals that year, Kobe Bryant shot a frustrating 4 out of 20 from the field in Game 6. The Indiana Pacers jumped on the Los Angeles Lakers to win by 33 big points to force Game 6 in LA. They needed to survive at least one more game to keep their hopes up for a possible title against such a powerhouse team.

Once again, it was Shaquille O'Neal who carried the Lakers load in Game 6, hungry for a title that had eluded him in the 1995 Finals. Superman would finish with 41 points and 12 rebounds that game. Meanwhile, Bryant was still struggling from the field as the second option if Shaq was not available. He was merely 8 out of 27 from the field for 26 points. He did, however, have ten rebounds. He and O'Neal rallied in the fourth quarter to give the Lakers the win and the championship. The five free throws he hit in the final stretches of the game proved invaluable since LA only won the game by five points.

As Game 6 wrapped up, the Lakers defeated the Indiana Pacers 4-2 in the 2000 NBA Finals to capture the franchise's first NBA title since 1988 when Magic Johnson's Showtime Lakers won their back-to-back titles. Shaquille O'Neal would win MVP honors, but Kobe Bryant had put his stamp as one of the premier players in the NBA despite only averaging 15.6 points per game and a shooting percentage of just under 37 percent in the NBA Finals. Despite often being seen as a rider in the O'Neal truck that dragged the Lakers to the championship, Kobe Bryant's timely performances were the defining moments of the series.

Of course, Kobe Bryant had a lot of awe-inspired supporters during that championship run in 2000. As teammate Rick Fox said, Kobe Bryant was not the selfish kid that focused on making spectacular plays rather than the ones that would have been more efficient. The things that the teenage Kobe used to do to get the team in tough situations turned were no more as he focused on making plays that benefited the whole team.[ii]

For Phil Jackson, who never saw Kobe eye-to-eye, he believed that Kobe did not have his old selfish agenda since he was so hungry for the championship that season. He said that Bryant would try to contribute to the team in more ways than scoring and realized at a very young age that there were several more ways to become productive while incorporating the whole team.[ii] This was a Kobe Bryant who, at a very young age, was learning to be a mature superstar that desired more than anything to win. But his hunger would not stop at a single title.

The Second Title, Dominating the Playoffs

With the birth of a new dynasty came the accompanying birth pains. For the first time, a chink in the dynamic duo emerged. Kobe Bryant blasted Shaquille O'Neal for coming to the training camp out of shape. Sensing that his more talented sidekick could overtake him soon, Shaq demanded that the ball should run through him in the post on every possession. The result was a season-long tumultuous relationship that yielded a record with 11 fewer wins than the previous season.

Nevertheless, Kobe Bryant continued to grow as a superstar whose potential seemed endless as he kept improving, growing, and maturing. Because the Lakers lost several key scorers like Ron Harper and Glen Rice, Bryant's reputation as one of the premier perimeter players in the league earned him the role as the Lakers' primary go-to guy together with O'Neal.

Kobe Bryant would open the first 20 games of the season scoring at least 30 points in 12 of those outings. Those 12 games included five straight occasions when he scored at least 30 points. He would then score 43 points on December 1, 2000, before finishing the next two games with a total of 74 points on shooting percentages above 50%.

After those three spectacular scoring games, Bryant had first 50-point game of his career on December 6, 2000, in a losing effort to the Golden State Warriors, 125-122 in Oakland, California. It was an overtime game where Bryant played 51 total minutes and made 18 of 35 field goals for 51.4 percent and made all 13 of his free throws. He also collected eight assists, seven rebounds, two steals, and one block. With that performance, Bryant's reputation as a prime-time scorer only grew by the minute.

Bryant's scoring tirade that season would not end there. On December 17 in an overtime win over the Toronto Raptors, while matching up with Vince Carter, who was also regarded as one of the best shooting guards of that generation, Kobe would score 40 points on 14 out of 19 shooting from the field and 11 out of 11 from the foul stripe. Four days later, he torched the Houston Rockets on their home court with 45 big points on a remarkably impressive 20 out of 26 shooting from the field in one of the days where Bryant seemed like he could not miss from the floor.

On January 15, 2001, in one of Kobe Bryant's best all-around performances that season, he put up 26 points, 11 rebounds, and 11 assists in his first triple-double game of the season. His second would come a month later when he had 25 points, ten rebounds, and ten assists in a win versus the Charlotte Hornets, the team that had drafted and traded him away.

Nearly two months later after he scored above 50 points for the first time in his career, Bryant would get close to hitting that mark again after scoring 47 points in a 102-96 road win over the Cleveland Cavaliers on January 30, 2001. A good portion of those points came from making 23 of his 26 shots from the foul line.

Because of Kobe's monstrous scoring output throughout the whole season up to the point of the All-Star weekend, he came into the midseason classic as the league's leading scorer and as a starter for the Western Conference once again. With Bryant's scoring leadership and his team's superior size, the West were leading entering the fourth quarter until the Eastern squad capped off a run sparked by Allen Iverson, who would become the All-Star MVP and later the league MVP. Kobe Bryant finished with 19 points as the leading scorer in the Western All-Star team.

Unfortunately for Kobe Bryant, he could not keep up the savage scoring pace because minor injuries kept him from playing his best after the All-Star weekend. Bryant would only score above 30 points four more times from then on and would miss a total of 14 games that season. The majority of his missed time came late in March when a combination of hip, elbow, shoulder, and pinky injuries hounded him.

At the end of the 2000-01 season, Kobe Bryant averaged new career highs in points and assists as he normed 28.5 points and 5.0 assists together with his usual numbers of 5.9 rebounds and 1.7 steals. He was shooting 46.4% from the floor while leading the Lakers in shot attempts. He nearly led the team and the league in scoring if it was not for the injuries that slowed him down in the second half of the season. Bryant would be named to the All-NBA Second Team for the second time and to the All-Defensive Second Team.

Despite finishing with fewer wins than the 1999-2000 season, the Lakers still finished first in the Pacific Division with a record of 56-26 to earn the second seed in the conference. But the team peaked in the playoffs and lost one game en route to capturing back-to-back NBA titles. They were able to get a three-game sweep in the opening round of the Western Conference Playoffs over the Portland Trail Blazers, including scoring 25 points on a shooting percentage of 72.7 and seven assists on April 26, 2001. At that point in the season, it seemed like the Los Angeles Lakers were peaking at the right time and were seemingly unstoppable.

The defending champions would continue the onslaught in the second round of the playoffs as they met the Sacramento Kings, who were in a race with them for the Division title during the regular season. Despite having only one game separating them in the regular-season standings, the difference in dominance and team dynamics seemed large. The Lakers would not even break a sweat in sweeping them out of the playoffs.

While Shaquille O'Neal remained the same dominant force that had led the Lakers in scoring throughout the playoffs, Kobe Bryant was the leading man against the Kings and was virtually unguardable in four games. He had 29 and 27 in the first two games before going into Sacramento with 36 points. Bryant would then wrap up the series by putting up 48 points and 16 rebounds in Game 4 as the Lakers swept the Kings out of the playoffs. Throughout that four-game series, Bryant averaged 35 points and nine rebounds as the most dominant perimeter player the league had at that time.

Kobe Bryant's dominance as an electrifying scorer continued in the Western Conference Finals. The Lakers would dominate the rest of the playing field en route to another sweep. Kobe was the catalyst in Game 1 of that series against the highly-touted San Antonio Spurs. After scoring 48 in the closeout against the Kings, Bryant would deliver 45 points and ten rebounds in their opening win versus the Spurs. Once again, he was virtually unstoppable en route to a shooting clip of 54.3% from the field in that 14-point win.

After that performance, the conversation about Kobe Bryant's place as one of the best, if not the best, players in the league would only grow to his advantage. Shaq, who was considered the best player of the Lakers back then, would even claim that Kobe was the most dominant force in the league by far even though guys like Tim Duncan, Allen Iverson, Kevin Garnett, Tracy McGrady, and Jason Kidd were all in their prime years.[ii]

On the other side of the court, San Antonio Spurs guard Antonio Daniels compared the experience of guarding Bryant to guarding Jordan. He would say that Kobe was like Mike in such a way that you just hoped they missed their shots even after you tried to play the best defense possible on them. And, in the words of then-Laker Horace Grant, who had a chance to play with Michael Jordan for three championships, "He's playing like No. 23. And he's only 22. That's scary." [ii]

But Coach Gregg Popovich of the Spurs made the best remark about Bryant's performance in that game. According to him, Kobe was no longer playing on talent alone but was very aware of the situations, his place, and where his teammates are.[ii] At only 22 years old, Bryant already had the IQ and the feel that the older veterans did not even have.

Despite seeing better defenses in Game 2, Kobe Bryant would still post 28 points, seven rebounds, and six assists on his way to helping his team win another game against the Spurs. In Game 3, Bryant would mince the Spurs defense yet again on his way to 36 points, nine rebounds, and eight assists in what would end up as a 39-point win. And, as the dust settled down in another blowout win in Game 4, Kobe Bryant finished with 24 points and 11 assists. All in all, he averaged 33.2 points against the San Antonio Spurs in the West Finals on his way to another appearance in the NBA championship round.

After that remarkable high-assist game from Kobe in that closeout game, Phil Jackson could not help but compare him to Michael once again. He said that, during his days of coaching Jordan, he allowed the man to be whatever player he would want to be as he avoided giving him roles. It was the same treatment with Kobe. Though Jackson had high expectations for Kobe, who exceeded them all by far, the young Laker guard did not have a particular role for the team. Whether he wanted to score, rebound, or assist was up to him.[ii] And in that closeout game against the Spurs, he wanted to play the role of facilitator.

The Los Angeles Lakers, thanks to the dominant outputs of both Kobe Bryant and Shaquille O'Neal all postseason long, were undefeated in 11 games heading into the NBA Finals. On the other side of the ring were the Philadelphia 76ers led by the 2001 MVP Allen Iverson, who was regarded as probably the best guard in the NBA.

With the rest of the team playing great defense on Kobe and with Iverson putting up 48 big points in Game 1, the Philadelphia 76ers managed to pull the upset of the century. They were the only team to beat the Los Angeles Lakers in the postseason that year. Kobe Bryant would finish with his worst game during that playoffs, only mustering 15 points on 7 out of 22 shooting from the field.

Intent on avoiding another poor shooting output, Bryant would methodically punish his defenders in Game 2 as he shot 11 out of 23 from the field against the tight Sixers defense on his way to 31 points, eight rebounds, and six assists. With the series tied 1-1 heading into Game 3, Bryant put up 32 points on another spectacular scoring night in the Finals.

And while defenses were taking away his good looks from the field in Game 4, Kobe would play the role of a facilitator very well. He finished with nine assists. He only shot 13 field goals for a total of 19 points while also grabbing ten rebounds using his excellent athletic abilities. In Game 5, Bryant would close the series out by putting a stat line of 26 points, 12 rebounds, and six assists as the Los Angeles Lakers won the final four games of the series after dropping Game 1. With that win and amidst the alleged alpha dog quarrels between Kobe and Shaq, the Los Angeles Lakers were champions of the basketball world for a second straight season.

Wrapping Up the Three-Peat

Kobe Bryant, entering the sixth season in the league at the tender age of 23 years old, had done things not even 32-year-old players have done in their career. Kobe was already a three-time All-Star, a two-time All-NBA and All-Defensive nominee, and a two-time NBA champion. At that point in his career, he no longer had anything to prove or achieve in the NBA to cement his legacy as a young star. However, Bryant still wanted more to quell his hunger for greatness. He still wanted to remain a champion and supreme force in the league.

The following season became Kobe's healthiest by far. He was able to play in 80 regular season games for the first time in his career. His scoring average dropped to 25.2, yet he had his best field goal shooting percentage of his career at 46.9 percent.

Despite a slight decline in his scoring average, Bryant was arguably at the finest he has ever been in his six-year NBA career, even as stories of feuds between him and Shaq grew.

Kobe Bryant started where he had left off the previous season as he scored in bunches in the outset of the 2001-02 season. The Lakers went on a 7-0 run at the start of the season, and Kobe scored at least 30 points in three outings, which included a 39-point output against the Utah Jazz on November 1, 2002, and a 38-point game against the very same team three days later.

Against the Clippers on November 20, Bryant had his first double-double game as a facilitator when he collected 25 points and 12 assists in a win. A night later, he had 24 points, 13 rebounds, and seven assists in a blowout win over the Denver Nuggets. While Kobe did not have any huge scoring explosions during the early parts of the season, he did maintain consistent outputs and occasionally figured above 25 points. He would tie his season high of 39 points in a losing effort against the Golden State Warriors on December 26.

After nearly three months of having no games of scoring above 40 points, Bryant surpassed his previous career-high in points with 56 in a blowout win on January 14, 2002, at home against the Memphis Grizzlies, 120-81. He made 21 of 34 shots from the field (61.8 percent) while making 11 of 12 free throws. He also added five rebounds, four assists, and one steal for good measure.

Among the other strong numbers that Bryant was able to collect through his long season was his first triple-double on February 12, 2002, against the Washington Wizards. He scored 23 points and made 15 assists while collecting 11 rebounds in the 103-94 victory. After that game, he had two more consecutive outings of double-digit assists.

Bryant would earn his first of four Most Valuable Player awards from the annual All-Star Game. His 31 points would help the Western Conference defeat the Eastern Conference 135-120 on February 10, 2002, at the First Union Center in Philadelphia, Pennsylvania. Amidst the jeers of the Philadelphia crowd, who he had insulted back in the NBA Finals, Bryant thrived in the negativity to make his hometown crowd suffer one of his best All-Star Game performances.

The feud between Bryant and O'Neal that shook the Lakers' dynamic duo the previous season did not show up in this season. The Lakers finished second to the Sacramento Kings in the Pacific Division and would take the third seed overall in the Western Conference Playoffs with a record of 58 wins and 24 losses. For the first time in what would be 11 occasions, Bryant was named to the All-NBA First Team. He was also named to the All-Defensive Team for the second year in a row.

Kobe and the Lakers had little trouble in the early round of the playoffs after sweeping the Portland Trail Blazers, once again, in a best-of-five series. Bryant averaged 26 points per game as well as 5.7 rebounds and five assists in those three games. His best effort in that series was his 34-point output in Game 1 as he torched the Blazers from the foul line.

The Lakers were equally dominant in the conference semifinals against the San Antonio Spurs and winning the best-of-seven series in five games. Bryant averaged 26.2 points per game and a similar 45.5 field goal percentage from the opening round. One of his best games was the series-clinching win on May 14, 2002, when Los Angeles won at home, 93-87. He would score 26 points on 10 of 20 shots from the field and eight rebounds with five assists. Again, the Spurs would have no answer for Kobe all series long, the same way they could not stop him in the past two seasons.

The cake walk ended as the Lakers faced a brick wall against Chris Webber's, Peja Stojakovic's, and Vlade Divac's Sacramento Kings in the Western Conference Finals that went all seven games. Bryant's scoring average went up in this series with 27.1 points per game on 41.9 percent shooting from throughout the field. He also averaged about 6.3 rebounds, 3.9 assists and 1.4 steals per game. Facing the defense of perimeter stopper Doug Christie, Kobe Bryant tried his mightiest to torch the Kings every single night despite facing a tougher cover from the previous two series.

The series included Robert Horry's great Game 4 buzzer-beater which tied the series at 2-2 apiece instead of trailing 1-3 with Game 5 in Sacramento. Although the Kings would win Game 5, Bryant averaged 30.5 points, 10.5 rebounds, and six assists in the final two games of the series to complete a come-from-behind 4-3 series win over the Kings. Bryant had 31 points and 11 rebounds in Game 6 in Los Angeles on May 31, 2002, in a 106-102 win. This was followed by another 30 points along with ten rebounds and seven assists in the 112-106 Game 7 victory on June 2, 2002, at the ARCO Arena in Sacramento, California.

In the Finals, a red-hot Lakers squad swept the New Jersey Nets and captured their third consecutive NBA title. Bryant would average 26.8 points per game with 51.4 field goal percentage and 54.5 percent from behind the three-point arc. His best game of the NBA Finals was scoring 36 points on June 9, 2002, at

New Jersey while collecting six rebounds, four assists, and two blocked shots.

The Lakers would become the first team since 1953-1954 to accomplish a three-peat. But it was not just the Lakers who achieved a three-peat as Shaquille O'Neal was Finals MVP for the third straight season. While Los Angeles celebrated their third consecutive title, little did they know that it would be the last for this core, which for now, seemed an impossible force to defeat – similar to the Chicago Bulls from the 1990s.

Chapter 5: Falling Out of the Kobe-Shaq Tandem

The Beginning of the End of a Dynasty

After three straight NBA championships, the Los Angeles Lakers of that era seemed like a dynasty that could not be stopped, especially with how they had the most dominant duo assembled in all of basketball. Kobe Bryant and Shaquille O'Neal were both the best players at their respective positions. Unfortunately for the Lakers, they were also both alpha dogs whose egos clashed with one another. While they had the potential to win several more titles as a duo, there was no stopping the inevitable falling-out period of the two most dominant forces in the league.

Fresh off three title wins and three dominant performances in the past three NBA Finals, Shaquille O'Neal decided that he needed rest and leisure in the offseason of 2002 after believing he deserved the time off. Whether O'Neal earned the leisure or not was out of the questions since he was 30 years old at that point and was entering the down years of his career. Moreover, his injury history and size could not take more grind than what it took in the last three NBA seasons. That was what angered Kobe Bryant.

O'Neal was suffering a toe injury throughout the 2001-02 season and could have had surgery to fix it in the offseason of 2002. However, he never did have the surgery until training camp was about to start, believing he needed to rest and that his rehabilitation period needed to start on company time since his injury happened while playing for the Lakers sometime in the past season.

Kobe never liked how O'Neal handled the injury. Ever the maniacal hard worker, Bryant believed that Shaq should have had the toe injury fixed as soon as possible to have him ready, healthy, and in shape as soon as the season started. For Kobe, there should have been no off-nights to stay on top of the NBA since the rest of the league was coming after them. He would always berate Shaq for coming into training camp fat and out of shape while he was off training to get better during the offseason.

Shaq's neglect of his health not also the reason why the feud was getting hotter between two of the NBA's premiere stars. Since the two stars teamed up in 1996, O'Neal was always the top dog of the franchise. He was the first option, no matter who the coach was, what situation they were in, and against any opponent they were up against. Meanwhile, Bryant was still the second choice in the majority of those years up until the time they won three straight titles.

In the midst of the title-chasing and dynasty-forming, Kobe Bryant improved to the point that he was becoming just as talented, if not better, than Shaquille O'Neal was. He even had more shot attempts during the regular seasons of their last two championship seasons. Bryant was becoming more aggressive and self-aware of his growing skills. At that point in their respective careers, Bryant was no longer choice B. He and O'Neal were both the top options on offense despite the fact that Kobe was still being treated as the Robin to Shaq's Batman.[viii]

Despite the feud, business went on and the season had to start whether Shaq was ready or not. As usual, Kobe Bryant was willing to compete at any given time since he was so amazing on a personal note at the start of the season. Kobe would start the first five games of the season with five double-doubles, which included two back-to-back triple-doubles. The first one was when he had 33 points, 15 rebounds, and 12 assists in a win against the Clippers on November 1, 2002. Two nights later, he had 33 points, 14 rebounds, and 12 assists against the Portland Trail Blazers in another win.

Running on a one-man team led by Bryant, nobody could blame the young star for trying to carry the load all by his lonesome even to the detriment of the Lakers, who struggled without O'Neal at the start of the season. One case in point was when Kobe scored 41 points in a loss to the Boston Celtics on November 7. Bryant had 47 shot attempts in that game. More than a week later, he shot 40 attempts again as he scored 45 points in a win over the Warriors. In the next match, he was 18 out of 37 from the field for 46 points against the Houston Rockets in a loss.

As a one-man show, Bryant was fantastic. He would have four early triple-doubles and four games of at least 40 points. But even as Kobe Bryant was scoring above 30 points in seven of his first 20 outings to start the season, the Lakers seemed miserable and like a shell of their championship selves even as Shaquille O'Neal returned to the lineup. Los Angeles was merely 7-13 at that point of the season. They would even fall to as low as 11-19 in their first 30 games.

When the Los Angeles Lakers fell to a poor record after losing to the Sacramento Kings in their Christmas Day matchup, enough was enough for the three-time defending champions. Things quickly normalized even though Kobe continued to dominate possessions while Shaq was steadily returning to the form that got him three Finals MVP awards.

The Los Angeles Lakers would suddenly go back to their winning ways and look like the three-time defending champions after that wake-up call from the Kings. And even as they played team ball better than ever, Kobe Bryant still was not short of spectacular moments as he continued to carve his name as the league' premiere perimeter player. He even proved his mastery of the three-point shot as he made a record 12 out of 16 attempts from beyond the arc to score 45 points in a win against the Seattle SuperSonics on January 7, 2003. While that record would be tied by two players over the course of the next 13 seasons, no other player would break that record even as the NBA would see an influx of great shooters.

The Kobe Bryant rampage would begin late on January 29 when he scored 40 points against the Phoenix Suns in a win. He would follow that up two days later when he torched the Kings for 38 points in another good shooting night from the young star. From then on, Kobe Bryant just kept coming and coming as he would not score below 30 points in 16 straight games. Nine of those games included some of the most amazing scoring moments the league has ever seen.

Bryant would start things off by putting up 46 points in the Mecca of basketball as he almost singlehandedly defeated the New York Knicks on February 6. He then had 42 in only 32 minutes in a blowout win over the Nuggets before putting up 51 big points against the same opponents just a night after. Despite back-to-back losses to the Spurs and the Knicks in the next two games wherein he scored at least each, Bryant would welcome the Houston Rockets in Los Angeles by dropping 52 points on them. Over the course of the next three games, Kobe had 40, 40, and 41 against the Jazz, Blazers, and SuperSonics to complete a record unseen and unbroken.

As the dust settled, Kobe Bryant just scored at least 40 points in nine straight games for the Los Angeles Lakers even as he was playing alongside a fellow dominant scorer in Shaquille O'Neal. That record remains as the best nine-game run for any player in league history. And, in those 16 games where he scored at least 30 points every outing, Bryant averaged 40.4 points per game. Simply put, Kobe Bryant was nothing short of special at that moment in time. Moreover, the Lakers would only lose three out of their next 19 games to become a contender in the West once more.

While Kobe Bryant, who was named an All-Star starter yet again, would not repeat the same rampage as the season was nearing its end, he did put up a season high of 55 points on 15 out of 29 shooting from the field against the Washington Wizards on March 28. He made nine three-pointers in that game. That would be his final matchup against Michael Jordan, who returned as Wizard for only two seasons but would soon retire at the conclusion of the season. Against the 39-year old great, Kobe showed his quality as the heir apparent as he torched Mike's defense and mercilessly defeated the man he was often compared to.

Bryant would end his final game of the regular season with 44 points in a win over the Golden State Warriors. At the regular season's conclusion, Kobe Bryant averaged 30 points, which was second in the league behind Tracy McGrady, to go along with 6.9 rebounds, 5.9 assists, and 2.2 steals. He was first in the league for most total points scored in the season and was nominated to the All-NBA First Team and the All-Defensive First Team. He even finished third in MVP voting behind Tim Duncan and Kevin Garnett. At that moment, nobody could argue that Kobe Bryant had just reached the level reserved for the most elite players in the league. He might not even be the Robin to Shaq's Batman as he was arguably the heart and soul that kept the Lakers going that season even as they struggled to reach the playoffs with a 50-32 record.

Bryant would open the postseason scoring 39 points over the Minnesota Timberwolves in Game 1. His Lakers would lose the next two games to fall 1-2 in the series even as Bryant combined for an output of 57 points in those two games. Nevertheless, Kobe bounced back in the next three games to lead his Lakers to victory and past the Timberwolves in six games. Against the Wolves, he averaged 31.8 points as he scored above 30 in all but one game.

Kobe Bryant's scoring tirade continued to the second round against the San Antonio Spurs, who they were so used to beating in the past few postseasons. However, the Spurs were out to prove they were the superior team that season as they beat the Lakers in the first two games where Bryant was still at his finest. Kobe averaged 32 points in those losses.

Bryant bounced back in Games 3 and 4 at home. In Game 3, he had 39 points as he made the free throw line his home. He made 17 of his 19 foul shots in that match. As the Lakers were looking to tie the series two wins apiece in the next game, Kobe Bryant would have 35 points, seven rebounds, and three assists to help his team win and even the series up.

However, the Lakers lost a crucial Game 5 match-up to the San Antonio Spurs after Big Shot Robert Horry uncharacteristically missed a game-winning three-pointer. Horry had been hitting game-winner after game-winner throughout his career, but that single miss led to the team's demise and eventual elimination in Game 6. The Spurs would go on to win the NBA title that season.

It was the end to the three-season championship streak for the Los Angeles Lakers, who were one of the few teams in league history to ever three-peat. While fingers were pointing to Kobe's emerging ego clashing with Shaq's, nobody could ever discount the effort that Bryant put up all season long especially as he led the Lakers in scoring and as he piled up historically numbers still unbroken. He was even the gear that kept the Lakers going after injuries and personal matters got in between their goal of winning a fourth straight title.

But even as Kobe and Shaq remained their dominant selves throughout the 2002-03 season, which ended poorly for the former three-time defending champions, it was still growing increasingly clear that the two alpha stars could not coexist any longer. On one part was a clear and established unstoppable force in O'Neal, who was aging but was still effective. On the other corner was a young and still improving star in Kobe Bryant out to become the leading man for the team. The worst part was that they were not even friends to begin with as Kobe would later admit.[vii]

The world, however, seemed prophetic when they suggested and predicted that the tandem, no matter how dominant it has become, will soon find its end. David Plotz of the Slate, proposed as early as 2001 that the dominant tandem would be unmade not because of on-court reasons but because of the massive egos their two best players. He said that both Bryant and O'Neal were too proud of themselves to play second to anybody.[ii]

Derek Fisher, also in 2001, had noticed along with Phil Jackson that nothing they ever did got the two superstars to get along. The Lakers were so focused on winning and taking shortcuts on their way to a dominant three-peat that they forgot about the personal relationships and the chemistry that should have been built between Kobe Bryant and Shaquille O'Neal.[ii]

Despite the turmoil and the increasingly failing relationship between Kobe and Shaq, the two superstars would have to outgrow their egos for at least one more season if they wanted to win more titles together. And, in that one season, they would find backup in familiar faces that were just as legendary as they were in their respective primes

The Laker Super Team, the Final Days of the Los Angeles Duo

Dethroned, the Lakers sought to rebound big time in 2004 by adding future Hall-of-Famers Karl Malone and Gary Payton to their already very formidable line-up during the off-season. With a star studded line-up, the Lakers were touted to romp away with the Larry O' Brien trophy despite the off-court troubles of Kobe Bryant who had a sexual assault case filed against him before the season began.

The new additions Malone and Payton are two of the best players at their respective positions. However, they never won championships in their prime years as a familiar name in Michael Jordan had always foiled their best chances at winning a title. Now, in Los Angeles, they were teaming up with Kobe Bryant, the man closest to Jordan in the history of basketball.

With three of the best players that ever played the by his side in one team and backed by some of the best role players available at that time, Kobe Bryant was almost sure to win a fourth NBA title in a span of only five years. And while he would have to share possessions and shot opportunities with O'Neal, Payton, and Malone, Kobe was still playing both ends of the court at a superstar's pace that season.

As the Los Angeles Lakers enjoyed a good opening month losing only three games in November, Kobe Bryant never had to score explosively compared to the amazing scoring outputs he was putting up a year ago without any other scorer with him in the team. He would only score above 30 points twice. His best in November were the 37 points he had in a winning effort against the defending champions San Antonio Spurs in his fourth game of the season.

It would take until the new year when Kobe Bryant would have a signature high-scoring game. On January 4, 2004, Bryant scored 44 points on 14 out of 27 shooting while also grabbing 10 rebounds for the Lakers, who were on a mini losing skid as Karl Malone was out with an injury and would not return until March.

Unfortunately for Bryant, he would miss several games late in January due to the shoulder injury he suffered in the offseason and to court appearances relating to the charges against him. Nevertheless, Kobe would still see the All-Star Game for the sixth overall time in his eight-year career. And right after the midseason classic, he would go back to work as he scored at least 30 points in five of his next six games. One of those games included a 40-point output against the Phoenix Suns as he shot 15 out of 25 in that win. On February 28, he had his first triple-double of the season when he had 25 points, 14 rebounds, and 10 assists against the Wizards in a win. He would have double digit assists in the next two games after that performance.

As soon as Karl Malone returned to injury on March 12, the Lakers would mount an 11-game winning streak that ended on April 2 thanks to the all-around team effort led by Bryant, who was already the Lakers' leading scorer at that juncture of the season. Kobe would have five games of scoring at least 30 points in those 11 wins. He would then score 45 in his second to the last game of the season. And, in the Lakers final game of the regular season, Bryant hit two buzzer-beating three-pointers against the Portland Trail Blazers. He made the first one to send the game into overtime, and the second one was to win the game.

At the end of the regular season, Kobe Bryant's numbers decreased from the previous season due to the presence of several other capable teammates. He averaged 24 points, 5.5 rebounds, 5.1 assists, and 1.7 steals in 65 appearances for the Lakers, who went on to win 56 games during the regular season. Again, Kobe was All-NBA First Team and All-Defensive First Team that season.

Kobe and company would bring their super team prowess into the playoffs to dominate the rest of the playing field. In the first round, they would have no trouble beating the Houston Rockets in five games despite subpar performances from Kobe Bryant in three of those outings. Nevertheless, he had 36 points in Game 2 while finishing things off with 31 points, 6 rebounds, and 10 assists in Game 5.

Coming into the second round, the Lakers would meet their tormentors from a season before. The defending champions the San Antonio Spurs still sported the same lineup that had won them the title just a little under a year before meeting the Los Angeles Lakers in the second round of the 2004 playoffs. They would not find any trouble beating the Lakers in Games 1 and 2, and it seemed like it would be a repeat of the previous season all over again.

Somehow, the Lakers would win Game 3 at home before Kobe Bryant erupted for 42 big points to help his team tie things up two wins apiece in Game 4. Thanks to the all-around performances and contributions of all four Laker stars, Los Angeles was able to win Games 5 and 6 to proceed to the Western Conference Finals for the fourth time in five years.

In Game 1 of the West Finals against the Minnesota Timberwolves, Bryant would focus on feeding the ball to Shaq since the big man had the clear advantage over the Wolves' frontline. Kobe would finish with only 23 points, but had 6 assists in that win. Despite a better performance from Bryant in Game 2, the Wolves tied the series up at one win each.

Uncharacteristically of Kobe Bryant, he would only attempt 12 shots in Game 3, but drew foul after foul to score 22 points, which included 10 from the foul stripe. It was Gary Payton who came up big in that game to give the lead back to the Lakers. Then, in what was Bryant's best performance of the series, he would torch the Wolves for 31 points to make it a commanding 3-1 lead for LA. The Lakers would only drop one of the next two games to advance as the favorites in the NBA Finals.

The clear-cut favorites heading into the 2004 Finals were the Los Angeles Lakers as they had the championship experience, the veteran leadership, and the All-Star appearances. Moreover, the veteran duo of Malone and Payton were both hungry to win the title that had long eluded them both. With all the pieces set for the Lakers to win one more title, only one thing could stop them from claiming their fourth championship—the massive ego rift between Kobe Bryant and Shaquille O'Neal.

Swarmed by the excellent inside defense of the tough-minded Detroit Pistons, Shaquille O'Neal's possessions were limited in Game 1 even though he finished with 34 points on more than 80% shooting. With O'Neal struggling to get possessions, it was Kobe Bryant who tried to put the team on his back to the detriment of the Lakers. Kobe would take 27 shots—nine more than Shaq did. However, the Detroit Pistons' perimeter defense was just as tough, and Bryant would only connect on 10 shots to score 25 in that loss for the Lakers. On his part, Kobe did not even try to get his other teammates going. He and Shaq were the only Lakers to score above 5 points.

Sporting the same two-man show of Kobe and Shaq in Game 2, the Lakers managed to force overtime and win it all by outscoring the Pistons by eight points in the extra period. Bryant led the way with 33 points while O'Neal had 29. Once again, Kobe dominated the possessions and none of the other Lakers were even able to score in double digits.

The two-man show would finally meet its defensive match. Neither Kobe nor Shaq could hit any of their attempts en route to a big blowout loss in Game 3. With only 68 points, it was uncharacteristic for the Lakers to have scored so low despite having so much firepower. Bryant and O'Neal would combine for only 25 points in that loss. The Pistons would extend the series lead to 3-1 as Kobe kept shooting blanks in Game 4 to put a waste to Shaq's 36 points and 20 rebounds.

Smelling blood and intent on stopping O'Neal from dominating the paint, the Pistons would limit the dominant big man to only 20 points on 13 shots in Game 5 as they allowed Kobe Bryant to try and take over. But even so, Bryant was shooting blanks and would not even try to pass the ball despite facing a swarm of Detroit defenders. He shot 7 out of 21 from the floor for only 24 points as the bad chemistry between Bryant and O'Neal forced the Lakers to cede the 2004 NBA title to the Detroit Pistons.

The End of a Dynasty

The loss to the Detroit Pistons and the implosion of the Kobe-Shaq tandem led to a domino effect that would shatter the foundations of the championship team the Lakers had sported since 1999. But overall, it was the immature and massive ego of Kobe Bryant that led to the downfall of a dynasty.

Kobe was a free agent entering the 2004 offseason while Phil Jackson's contract had just expired. The Los Angeles Lakers, however, would not tender an extension to Jackson. The latter said that he would not return to the team if Bryant were still around. While the media was focused on how Kobe could not coexist with Shaq in the same team, his deteriorating relationship with Jackson was also a side story worthy of being told over and over again.

At an age and skill level where Kobe could dominate the league as a member of any other team, he was deeply frustrated with how Jackson's offensive scheme, the triangle offense, focused more on Shaq as the centerpiece. Bryant was at the height of his athletic prowess and was only getting better with hard work and experience. He believed that he should have been the focus of the attack. Bryant was vocal about that with Phil.

Other than his frustration with how the Laker offense was focused on Shaquille O'Neal, Kobe Bryant thought that their system was so simple that it did not give him a full chance to display the peak and potential of his talents. Jackson would try to calm Kobe down by telling him that their system was the most efficient way they could win titles. But Bryant was still displeased and felt that his talents were underutilized.[ii]

With Kobe wanting to be the central piece of the offense, the star guard would often play outside the flow of the system so that he could score the ball on his own while displaying the full array of his offensive repertoire. Instead of doing it the easy and right way, he would isolate himself from everyone else so that he could try to put on a show. Phil Jackson was not too happy about that side of Kobe. In his book, he would even call Kobe Bryant the most uncoachable player in the league.

As soon as the 2003-04 season ended, Phil Jackson would give Laker general manager Mitch Kupchak an ultimatum—it was a choice between him and Kobe. Jackson told the front office that he would not return the following year if Bryant were still around. He was so frustrated with the fact that Kobe would not listen to anybody and would even sabotage offensive sets just to try and play hero ball.[ii] The Lakers, wanting to build the team around the younger and more talented Kobe Bryant, would not give into Phil Jackson's demands. They would not extend the Zen Master's contract.

Shaquille O'Neal was not so keen on the idea of ditching Phil Jackson. He was very fond of Phil as a coach and mentor. He was getting uneasy with how the Lakers were heading in a direction he did not like. Shaq felt like he was not getting the proper treatment from the front office as they were leaning towards Kobe's demands. Because of that, he demanded a trade.[ix]

While O'Neal was on his way to the Miami Heat in a trade that sent Lamar Odom, Caron Butler, and a first-round pick, among others, Kobe Bryant re-signed with the Lakers and had hoped to mature himself up and try to win more titles with Shaq.

However, it was all too late as the big man was set to join the Heat and team up with another young shooting guard in Dwyane Wade.

While much of the blame gravitated towards Kobe's alleged selfishness, massive ego, and immaturity, Bryant would later defend himself. He said that he had a choice back then to join a different franchise and play like the franchise superstar he truly was while averaging above 35 points per game. However, he swallowed his ego just to team with Shaq again.[ii] But it never came to be. The dynasty ended just as predicted—due to the roster implosions.

Chapter 6: The Down Years

First Season as a Lone Star in LA

After the downfall of the Laker dynasty, all that remained was the 26-year-old star guard named Kobe Bryant. Phil Jackson was gone, Shaq was over in Miami, Payton and Fisher had moved on to other teams, and Karl Malone had retired as second in most points scored in a career. Bryant was all alone leading a team of role players and young talents. Though he always wanted to be the centerpiece of the franchise, he never wanted to alienate his teammates and coaches altogether. Nevertheless, it was business as usual. Bryant needed to man up and face the harsh reality that he was a lone star trying to carry a rebuilding franchise.

As predicted, Bryant shouldered the load for the Lakers all season long. He would have several remarkable performances early in the season and was putting up great numbers from all aspects of the game. Kobe would have 38 points at the beginning of his second game of the season. He then had 41 points against the Orlando Magic on November 12, 2004, before piling up a triple-double a week later against the Phoenix Suns. Bryant would then have 40 points against the Sacramento

Kings on November 26. Despite those numbers, Bryant was in the losing end of all of those games.

Kobe did, however, have victories in between losses while performing respectably as an all-around player. He had a triple-double in a win over the Golden State Warriors in December. While attempting only 12 shots, he finished with 10 points, 12 rebounds, and ten assists. Though it came in a losing effort, he did, however, have a triple-double in his next game against the Suns before torching the Clippers for 37 points.

As December was nearing its end, Kobe would score at least 40 points in three straight games. The first one was in a loss against the Miami Heat on Christmas Day in his first game ever against Shaq. He then had 48 on the Toronto Raptors as he shot 14 out of 26 from the field before wrapping it up with 42 points in a win over the Denver Nuggets in his first game of 2005.

Though Kobe would score in bunches all season long on his way to another All-Star appearance for the purple and gold, he would soon realize that it was lonely on top of the Laker food chain and that he alone could not lead his team to victories. Bryant would have five more games of scoring at least 40 points before ending the season without a playoff appearance for the first time in his career. He averaged 27.6 points, 5.9 rebounds,

6.0 assists, and 1.3 steals as well as being demoted to the All-NBA Third Team.

First Scoring Title, the 81-Point Masterpiece

For the first time in his career, Kobe Bryant was sitting at home alone watching sixteen teams squaring it off for the NBA title. After not making the postseason for the first time in his career, Kobe would have a long offseason full of personal meditation, reflection, hard work, and mending.

Mending would involve fixing his ties with Phil Jackson, who was re-hired in the offseason of 2005. The two multiple-time champions came to an understanding about their differences in philosophies and opinions. There were no more feuds between master and pupil as Bryant became more submissive to Jackson's teachings while the latter fully utilized the skills of the best shooting guard and possibly the greatest player of that era.

While Kobe was still struggling to lead a team of role players and borderline scrubs, the 2005-06 season was an overall test of his individual talents and leadership skills. Bryant would suffer through a whole season trying to drag teammates Smush Parker, Kwame Brown, Chris Mihm, and Luke Walton to make their

101

season competitive at the very least. His only capable teammate was versatile forward Lamar Odom.

Nevertheless, with Phil back on his side, Bryant's full potential as an individual once-in-a-generation talent was fully realized. He would open the 2005-06 season scoring above 33 points on four straight occasions. The Lakers would win three out of those four games. On November 16, 2005, Kobe then scored a then-season high of 42 against the New York Knicks before following it up with four more stellar scoring performances. He would score at least 40 points in the next four games before capping it all off with 46 points in a loss to the New Jersey Nets.

One of the best highlights of Kobe Bryant's season came on December 20 against the Dallas Mavericks. Shooting the lights out and obviously unconscious, Bryant would make 18 of his 31 field goal attempts and 22 of his 25 shots from the foul line to score a total of 62 points in only three quarters. Entering the fourth quarter, Bryant had outscored the entire Dallas Mavericks team by one point all on his own. However, he would only play 32 minutes as the Lakers had already blown the Mavs out. Kobe would not play a single minute in the fourth quarter to the dismay of fans, who thought that he could have exceeded even the greatest scoring games.

Fast forward to 2016, Kobe Bryant would fondly remember that great individual performance. When asked about his motivation, Bryant would say that it was Del Harris, who was an assistant with the Mavs back then. Kobe never liked Harris when the latter was his coach in 1996. Del Harris made him come off the bench for two seasons, but nevertheless made him earn his minutes. While thankful for Harris' mentorship and drive, Kobe nonetheless vowed revenge against his former coach. It was in the form of that 62-point game.[x]

Those 62 points were not his last outburst that season as Kobe continued to tear the league down with his scoring transcendence. It was not even his best that season; he would save his best for later. But, as the season went on, Bryant started a five-game streak of scoring at least 40 points. In the middle of all that was a game against the LA Clippers where he scored 50 points on 41 shots from the floor on January 7, 2006.

Bryant would then top that 50-point game by scoring 51 on the Sacramento Kings in a loss. He was 17 out of 35 from the field while shooting 13 out of 13 from the free throw line. Kobe would follow that performance up with 37 points in a loss to the Phoenix Suns. As good as those performances were, they were all preludes to what was going to be the most incredible scoring performance in NBA history.

Facing a game Toronto Raptors squad led by Chris Bosh and Jalen Rose, Kobe Bryant's Lakers were down by double digits entering the second of their game on January 22, 2006. Trying to bring his team back from the deficit, Kobe Bryant had already scored 26 points in the first two quarters and was rearing for one of his usual 40-point games or even a performance above 50 points. But he would exceed those expectations by a mile.

Attempting shot after shot in the third quarter just to try and keep his team competitive throughout what would seem like another impending loss for the Lakers, Kobe Bryant saw that every attempt he took went through the hoop. They were facing an 18-point deficit, but Bryant hit 11 field goals in the third quarter alone to close the gap. By the end of the quarter, the Lakers had completed a comeback and were ready to give the Raptors a fight in the fourth quarter. More interestingly, Bryant had already equaled his first half production. Kobe scored 27 points in the third quarter for a total of 54 entering the final canto. That was when history was made.

Kobe Bryant kept coming at the Raptors in the fourth quarter as the Lakers grabbed the lead and totally took over the game. However, Bryant's performance was the main story within the match as teammates regularly fed him the ball to watch history being unfolded. Bryant swished in perimeter jumpers, attacked the basket, and drew fouls as he was nearing the 80-point mark. At 79 points, Kobe Bryant heard the chants from the fans who wanted him to reach at least 80 points. He would draw a foul and complete an amazing 81-point game after swishing in both free throws to the "M-V-P" chants made famous by the Laker fans when watching Kobe attempting free throws. Bryant had just scored 55 points in the second half alone. And yes, he scored 81 points in a single game.

Lakers owner Jerry Buss would describe that performance as "a miracle unfolding in front of your eyes." Even teammates Devean George and Luke Walton could not believe the historic game that was happening before them as the latter would even have Kobe sign an autograph for him.[ii]

On the other bench, then-Raptors head coach Sam Mitchell and young outstanding big man Chris Bosh were thoroughly impressed and made believers by the show that the superstar guard was putting up that night. Jalen Rose and Mike James of the Raptors were even aware how hot Kobe was but failed to stop him nonetheless. They admitted that the whole team even went on to become cheerleaders.[ii] It was truly one great scoring night, and even their opponents had to shake their heads in awe and disbelief of what had happened before their very eyes.

By the numbers, Kobe Bryant hit 28 of his 46 field goal attempts for an unconscious 60.9% shooting clip from the floor. He made seven three-pointers and 18 out of his 20 free throw attempts in that game. With his 81-point total, Kobe Bryant surpassed Elgin Baylor's longtime Laker record of 71 points. He also moved up to second place in most points scored in a single game. Only Wilt Chamberlain's 100 points back in the 60's is ahead of Kobe's best single-game production.

While it is never to demean Wilt's incredible performance back in the day, many would argue that Kobe Bryant's 81-point outburst was just as good, if not better than the Stilt's historic performance. When Chamberlain hit the century mark, it was in a blowout game, and he was just trying to chase history. The Sixers were even intentionally fouling opposing players so that Wilt could get the ball back on the other end of the court. Comparing that to Kobe's performance, it was a close game until the fourth quarter when the Lakers gained the lead and never looked back. The Raptors were making it a close game as the LA Lakers needed Bryant to stay on the floor to win the bout for them.[xi] Kobe Bryant did not score 81 points because he wanted to. He did so because he had to.

At 7'1" and nearly 300 pounds, Wilt Chamberlain was built to dominate an era with undersized and un-athletic centers. He was a man among boys, the giant in Lilliput. Practically nobody could guard him in the paint because he was far taller, bigger, and stronger than all his defenders. You also add the fact that there was no three-second violation in the paint back when Wilt Chamberlain ruled the NBA. Hence, he could have camped out in the shaded lane long enough until he had good position.[xi]

In comparison to the era when Kobe scored 81 points, Bryant was up against defenders that were just as big as, or even bigger than, him. He was a perimeter player tasked with doing ball handling, running, and defending. Kobe had to expend more energy on both ends of the floor. You also add the fact that hitting perimeter shots is far more challenging a task than camping in the lane to dunk the ball over smaller defenders.[xi] And while Bryant's output was 19 points shy of Chamberlain's, nobody could discount that his performance was arguably the best that any individual player has put up in the long history of the NBA.

As the season went on, the highlight of the year for any player in the league would have to be the 81 points that Bryant had put up. He would not come close to reaching that mark again any time that season as the Lakers continued to fight for a playoff position. However, Bryant did register 14 more games of scoring at least 40 points on top of another All-Star start for him.

He would even score 50 or more points on two more occasions near the end of the season.

At the end of the regular season, Kobe Bryant secured his first scoring title after averaging an incredible 35.4 points. The last person to average at least 35 points per game was Michael Jordan back in 1988. Bryant also averaged 5.3 rebounds, 4.5 assists, and 1.8 steals en route to his return to the All-NBA First Team and All-Defensive First Team. More importantly, his team would get back to the playoffs after finishing the season with a record of 45 wins and 37 losses. Bryant, sadly, would only finish fourth in MVP voting behind Steve Nash, LeBron James, and Dirk Nowitzki.

The Los Angeles Lakers came into the playoffs in an unfamiliar state. They were the underdogs against the second-seeded Phoenix Suns. But despite their underdog status, they surprisingly played well enough to make it a tough series for one of the best regular-season teams in the NBA that season. Even though the Suns played tight defense on Kobe Bryant during the first three games, the Lakers were able to lead the series 2-1 heading into Game 4.

Game 4 in Los Angeles was a display of Kobe's primetime clutch prowess. In fact, it was one of his most memorable playoff performances. Though he struggled against the defense of Raja Bell all game long, Kobe Bryant managed to shake loose of his defender and forced overtime. In overtime, Bryant took the ball near midcourt as the clock was winding down with the Suns up by a point. Bryant dribbled the ball to the attack zone and suddenly rose up for a midrange jumper over several defenders to drill the clutch shot and win the game for the Lakers, who were up 3-1 at that point against the Phoenix Suns.

However, the Lakers eventually faded as the Suns went back to the form that helped them get the second seed in the West. They would blow the Lakers out in Game 5. In Game 6, all the stars seemed set for a Laker upset as Bryant scored a new career playoff high of 50 points. He made 20 of his 35 field goal attempts in that game. However, the Suns forced and won overtime in what was the final chance for the Los Angeles purple and gold to win the series. The Lakers would lose by 31 points in Game 7 as what seemed like a David versus Goliath match ended in favor of the giant.

Second Scoring Title, Losing to the Suns Again

Kobe Bryant came into the 2006-07 season sporting the same weak supporting cast but with the same skillset that had made him the deadliest weapon in the NBA for the past few seasons.

However, he did not sport the same number as he changed his jersey number from 8 to 24, saying that he had always wanted that number, but it was taken when he first arrived in the league.

As early as November 30, 2006, Kobe Bryant would produce his first 50-point game out of a total of ten that season. In a 30-point blowout win over the Utah Jazz, Bryant arguably could have had more than the 52 points he scored had he played more than the 34 minutes he played. Kobe hit 19 of his 26 attempts in that game while converting 12 out of 15 shots from the charity line. Fifteen days later, he would top that season high by putting up 53 points together with ten rebounds and eight assists for a near triple-double effort in a double-overtime win over the Houston Rockets.

Though it came in a losing effort against the Charlotte Hornets, Kobe Bryant scored a new season high of 58 points on December 29 as he made 22 of his 45 field goal attempts. He would then start 2007 on a good note when he torched the Sacramento Kings for 42 points, ten rebounds, and nine assists for another near triple-double.

While Kobe Bryant was already so impressive in his first two months that season, his best efforts came near the tail end of the regular campaign after seeing the ninth selection to the midseason classic where he won the MVP award for the second time. He had 31 points, six assists, and six steals in the All-Star Game to bag the best player of the game award.

The Lakers would, however, enter a seven-game skid at the beginning of March as they were on the cusp of missing the playoffs. But a sudden Kobe Bryant explosion prevented that from happening when he scored a new season high of 65 points against the Portland Trail Blazers on March 16 in an overtime win. Bryant hit 23 of his 39 field goal attempts and converted eight three-pointers. But Kobe would not stop with his 65 points.

Two days after registering his new season high, Kobe Bryant would score 50 against the Minnesota Timberwolves in a win for the Lakers. On March 22, he then delivered his second 60-point game of the season when he hit 20 of his 37 field goal attempts in a win over the Memphis Grizzlies. Because of that performance, Bryant became the first player since Michael Jordan in 1987 to record three consecutive games of scoring at least 50 points.

Bryant was not content with equaling Jordan's output as he delivered 50 points against the New Orleans Hornets a game after his 60-point outburst. After that performance, Kobe became the only other player to score 50 or more points in four consecutive games. The other player was Wilt Chamberlain, who did it about 40 years before. As an encore of sorts, Kobe ended a five-game winning streak for the Lakers by posting 43 points against the Golden State Warriors.

Kobe Bryant was not done posting high scoring numbers as the end of the regular season was nearing. He would score 53 on the Rockets in a losing effort on March 30. He scored 50 on the Clippers in another loss before scoring the same number of points against the Sonics on April 15 just when the season was about to end.

Kobe Bryant would average 31.6 points, 5.7 rebounds, 5.4 assists, and 1.4 steals on his way to another First Team nomination in the All-NBA and All-Defensive selections. He would win his second scoring title and finished third in the MVP voting behind Nowitzki and Nash. And with his leadership leading a bunch of role players, the Lakers won 42 games to qualify for the playoffs again.

Sadly, their first round matchup with the Phoenix Suns was a lot less competitive compared to last season as they were defeated easily in five games. In the Lakers' lone win in that series, Bryant finished with 45 points and averaged 32.8 points, 5.2 rebounds, and 4.4 assists in the five games he played in another early postseason exit for him and his squad. Despite the three post-Shaq years wherein he and the Lakers struggled, things quickly turned for the better as things shook up for the purple and gold team in the next season.

Chapter 7: Bryant's Return to Glory

The MVP Season, Return Trip to the NBA Finals

Frustrated by all the first round exits and the weak supporting cast surrounding him, Kobe Bryant would hold the whole Los Angeles Lakers organization ransom by demanding a trade if things did not shape up for the better. Kobe, on a radio show, would even admit how frustrating it was being surrounded by scrub teammates and how he still wanted to be a Laker but was prevented from retiring as one because of the roster surrounding him.[ii] However, he would rescind the trade demand after talking with Phil Jackson and re-aligning their goals together as the two most significant members of the team back then.

While it was never clear what he and Jackson talked about, what was clear was that Kobe Bryant was suddenly a changed person after rescinding his trade demand and rejoining the Lakers in the hopes of making the team a lot better. Kobe was clearly making it a point to incorporate his teammates more on the offense while never failing to ignite their passion for winning.

In stark comparison to his previous two seasons, the only massive scoring explosion that Kobe had at the early part of the

114

season was his 45-point performance in the opening-day loss against the Rockets. Since then, he seemed more focused on playing within the flow of the game while making his teammates more confident every single night. The Lakers were 12-8 through their first 20 games and were only getting better as the season progressed.

The Lakers would suddenly find themselves on top of the Western Conference for most of the season as the campaign unfolded. They did so even as Kobe Bryant did not have those usual 40 or 50-point game the world had gotten so used to seeing from him over the past three seasons. Bryant was so aligned at winning games that numbers did not seem too important for him that season.

Nevertheless, Kobe still had great performances such as the 39 points, 11 rebounds, and eight assists he had over the New York Knicks in a win. That night was special for him as he became the youngest person in league history at that time to reach 20,000 points. That record has since been broken by LeBron James. Kobe followed that up with 38 points against the Suns on December 25. And as 2007 ended, LA found itself with an impressive 19-11 season record heading into 2008.

Kobe Bryant was the main person to thank for the improvement of the Los Angeles Lakers' dynamics despite having no real roster changes that would have impacted them that early. But the rise of Andrew Bynum as a legitimate starter and future impact star as well as Lamar Odom's continued consistency as an all-around player helped the team get the job done.

Not losing sight of his scoring ways, Kobe Bryant would score 48 points against the Seattle SuperSonics on January 14, 2008, as he made 21 of the 44 attempts he put up that night. Before that game, Bryant scored 37 points back-to-back in wins against the Bucks and the Grizzlies. Then, on January 21, Bryant showed a rare side to his game when he attempted only seven shots and focused on making his 11 assists in a win over the Denver Nuggets.

Despite the fact that Kobe Bryant was becoming the leader everyone desired him to be at that point of the season while maintaining his usual output on both ends of the floor, there was only so much that a lone superstar could do for the Lakers, who just lost starting center Andrew Bynum to a season-ending injury. In response to Bynum's fall and Kobe's demands of star-caliber teammates, the Los Angeles Lakers front office would make a trade that seemed like a steal at the time.

On February 1, 2008, the Los Angeles Lakers announced a trade that sparked the return of the team to its glory days. The Lakers received from the Memphis Grizzlies two-time All-Star and skillful power forward Pau Gasol in exchange for disappointing center Kwame Brown, several other role players, and the draft rights to the younger brother Marc Gasol. Pau would then form a formidable duo with Kobe Bryant, who has never had a big man as good as Gasol since his days with Shaq. On the day that the Lakers acquired the Spanish big man, Kobe scored a then-season high of 46 points in a win over the Toronto Raptors.

The addition of Pau Gasol to the lineup only made the LA Lakers more competitive than they already were that season. Gasol's skillset perfectly complimented Bryant's transcendent talents as the duo quickly adjusted to each other's tendencies and personalities. While Kobe was the dominant figure, Gasol was the soft-spoken one as the pair of All-Stars formed a friendship and chemistry that made the Lakers more formidable than ever.

Seeing less defensive attention focused on him, Bryant, who was the leading MVP candidate at the midpoint of the season, would score 52 points on the Dallas Mavericks in an overtime win on March 2. He made 15 of his 27 shots while converting 20 of his 27 charity line attempts. Bryant also had 11 rebounds in that game. That was not his final explosion as Kobe would score 53 points in what would become a losing effort against the rebuilding Grizzlies on March 28.

In what was the most important personal battle that Kobe had in the regular season, the leading MVP candidate would edge out fellow MVP candidate Chris Paul in their matchup on April 11. Kobe and his Lakers would beat CP3 and his Hornets to not only hand Bryant the lead in the MVP race, but leadership of the Western Conference as well. Bryant had 29 points, ten rebounds, and eight assists in that game.

Despite a slight drop-off in scoring and his failure to win a third consecutive scoring title, Kobe Bryant arguably had his best season as a leader with averages of 28.3 points, 5.2 rebounds, 6.3 assists, and 1.8 steals. Not only was he First Team in the All-NBA and All-Defensive selections, he was also the league MVP at the conclusion of the regular season. It was his first and only Most Valuable Player award as he led his team to a top finish in the West with a record of 57 wins against 25 losses.

With a balanced inside-outside attack, Kobe Bryant and Pau Gasol worked together perfectly to quickly sweep the Denver Nuggets out of the first round of the postseason. Kobe's best performance in that series was in Game 2 when he had 49 points and ten assists. He averaged 33.5 points in that round against the Denver Nuggets.

Showcasing the full capabilities of his offense, Bryant would lead his Lakers past the Utah Jazz in Game 1 of the second round with his 38 points on 8 out of 16 shooting from the field and 21 out 23 from the foul stripe. He followed that performance up with 34 points, eight rebounds, and six assists in Game 2 to lead the series 2-0.

Unfortunately, despite averaging 33.5 points in the next two games, Bryant's and his Lakers would find themselves in a tie with the Jazz, who beat them in Games 3 and 4. Kobe, however, would combine for 60 points in Games 5 and 6 to proceed to the Western Conference Finals for the first time since 2004. He averaged 33 points in that round against the Jazz.

Waiting in the West Finals were the defending champions the San Antonio Spurs, who Kobe had a lot of history with ever since his three-peat days back in the early part of the decade. Against the defense of veteran Bruce Bowen, Kobe seemed to struggle from the field for the first time in those playoffs as he averaged only 24.5 points in the first two games of the series. Despite's Bryant's struggles, the Lakers would win the first two meetings.

For the first time in the series, Bryant would score at least 30 points when the games moved over to San Antonio for the third and fourth installments. However, the Spurs managed to blow the Lakers out in Game 3. Banking on Kobe's 28 points and ten rebounds in Game 4, the Lakers made it a difficult 3-1 mountain to climb for the Spurs, who would go on to lose in five games after Kobe Bryant punished them with 39 points.

With that win against the San Antonio Spurs in five games in the Western Conference Finals, Kobe Bryant was on his way to the NBA championship round for the very first time since 2004 and without Shaquille O'Neal in the lineup. At that point, Shaq was already a four-time champ as he won a ring without Kobe in 2006. Kobe was itching to tie his former teammate and rival's hardware.

Unfortunately for Kobe and his Los Angeles Lakers, they were not the only ones hungry for a title. Kevin Garnett and Ray Allen would band together with Paul Pierce in Boston to make the Celtics legitimate title contenders and to relive the glory days that were once dominated by the rivalry between them and the Lakers. Marching into the Finals with the best record in the league, the Boston Celtics were going to be the biggest thorn in the side of Kobe Bryant as history was once again revived between the two most storied franchises in NBA history.

However, the stars were not aligned on the side of Kobe and his squad. The Celtics continued to punish them with three-pointers throughout the whole series while Garnett pushed Gasol in the paint as the latter earned a reputation for being a soft big man. And while Kobe Bryant was undoubtedly the best player in the world for several years already, he had no chance against three hungry NBA superstars that were still ringless.

The Celtics would go on to win Games 1 and 2. Bryant had his best performance in Game 3 when he had 36 points. However, he would see tougher cover and defenses throughout the next three games as the Celtics would win two more games capped off by the embarrassing 39-point loss that the Lakers suffered in Game 6. In the end, it was the Big Three of Pierce, Garnett, and Allen that hoisted the championship trophy while Kobe Bryant was left frustrated and angry at himself for the loss. Even today, Bryant admits that the 2008 Finals loss to the Celtics was the worst defeat he has ever had in the championship series. After that loss, he would vow to get back at them for robbing him of what could have been his fourth championship ring.

Fourth NBA Title, Return to the Top of the League

Hungry and determined to avoid another loss in the NBA Finals, Kobe Bryant and his Lakers came into the 2008-09 season with renewed vigor as the team had grown to become better with a core of All-Stars surrounded by experienced role players. Andrew Bynum and Trevor Ariza both returned from injury while Kobe and Pau had grown to become better acquainted with one another after a full offseason together.

With Kobe resolute to bring back the glory days of the Lakers, he would lead the team to a 7-0 start in the regular season, though he was not scoring as much as he used to. He was playing with a mangled right index finger that forced him to shoot with his left hand at times. Even so, he was able to lead the Los Angeles Lakers to a 17-3 record in the early juncture of the season as his leadership has reached heights it had never been before.

During those winning moments, Kobe Bryant was getting praises from all over the roster. Andrew Bynum would call the team unbeatable when Bryant was focused and moving the ball around the whole game. And, as assistant coach Brian Shaw said, Phil Jackson had learned to trust Kobe Bryant more than ever to the point that he would even let his superstar do what he felt was proper for them to win, even if it was not the play that the coaching staff drew up. The 2008-09 season was indeed the peak of Bryant's overall prowess.

As the season went on, Bryant would still have great individual performances, though he was focused more on team basketball. He would have a then-season high of 41 points in a narrow loss to the Orlando Magic on December 20. He would then welcome the New Year with 41 points on January 2, 2009, against the Utah Jazz. A week later, he had 36 points and 13 assists against the Indiana Pacers. Much later, he recorded his second triple-double of the season when he ran through the Clippers with 18 points, ten rebounds, and 12 assists. But the best was yet to come for Bryant.

On February 2, 2009, Kobe's 61 points became the highest scoring output in Madison Square Garden as part of a 126-117 win over the New York Knicks. Bryant had a shooting percentage of 61.3 and made half of his six shots from behind the three-point line. A portion of his points was due to making all 20 of his free throws. It was his highest-scoring performance of the season, followed by 49 points on March 1, 2009 – although it was a losing effort to the Phoenix Suns on the road,

118-111. Bryant also had 11 rebounds while making 18 of 38 from the field (47.4 percent) and all 10 of his foul shots.

What was even more entertaining than that game was the All-Star Game in Phoenix. That game marked the final that time that Shaquille O'Neal played in the midseason classic. It was also the last time he would team up with Kobe Bryant. Looking like the old Laker tandem, Bryant and Shaq relived the plays that made them a dominant tandem earlier in the decade. They were running give-and-goes and pick-and-rolls like there was no rift or animosity between them. And while Bryant would end up with 27 points to lead the West, O'Neal performed just as well as the most dominant duo in NBA history won co-MVP in the All-Star Game.

While Kobe Bryant would not have a lot of explosive scoring games after that performance in Madison Square Garden, he would remain the consistent presence that led the Lakers to one of their best seasons as a franchise. The purple and gold of Los Angeles seemed unbeatable as they earned the best record in the West behind Bryant's leadership. They finished with 65 wins and 17 losses.

Behind another great season for the Lakers was Kobe Bryant, who averaged 26.8 points, 5.2 rebounds, 4.9 assists, and 1.5

steals. Amazingly, he played all 82 games of the season while battling an injured right index finger. Always the competitor and fighter, he braved through the injury to be named to the All-NBA and All-Defensive First Teams yet again.

With the right chemistry for the peaking Los Angeles Lakers heading into the playoffs, there was almost no doubting that they were the favorites to win the coveted NBA title that season. And with the way they handled the Utah Jazz in the first round, it was almost inevitable that they were going to be the representatives of the Western Conference in the Finals.

Kobe and company would open up the playoffs by beating the Jazz soundly in the first two games wherein the Black Mamba scored 50 total points. After dropping Game 3 in Utah, Kobe would show no mercy as he beat the Jazz down with 38 points in Game 4 before finishing the series off with 31 points in Game 5. Both games were double-digit wins for the streaking Los Angeles Lakers.

The Lakers would face their toughest challenge of that season in the form of the Houston Rockets in the second round of the playoffs. For Kobe, it was also the most difficult challenge he would face as he would be swarmed by two top perimeter defenders in Ron Artest and Shane Battier. Though he would shake off the defense in Game 1 as he scored 32, LA would end up losing that one to the Rockets.

Games 2 and 3 were different as Bryant shrugged off the tough defensive looks that Artest and Battier were giving him. He would combine for 73 points in those two games as he scored 40 in Game 2 before helping his team get a 2-1 lead with his 33 points in Game 3. However, Houston would tie the series up with a 12-point win in Game 4.

Kobe Bryant would lead a huge Laker rally in Game 5 as they relentlessly attacked the defense, intent on not losing the series lead they had worked so hard on. In only 30 minutes of action, Bryant scored 26 points to lead his team to a 40-point win. However, competitive as they were, the Houston Rockets forced Game 7 by winning Game 6 by double digits. Though Kobe was limited to 14 points, which were his lowest for the whole postseason, the Los Angeles Lakers beat the Rockets down by 19 points to win Game 7 and proceed to the West Finals.

The Western Conference Finals was marketed as an offensive display between two teams that had a lot of firepower. It was also going to be a critical one-on-one show between two elite scorers in Kobe Bryant and Carmelo Anthony of the Denver Nuggets. Game 1 was indicative of that as the two transcendent scorers squared off in a shootout. Bryant, with 40 points, won the one-on-one battle and the game. However, Anthony and the Nuggets would not stay down as they beat the Lakers in Game 2 to tie the series.

For the second time in the series, Kobe Bryant would erupt for more than 40 points as he finished with 41 markers in Game 3 to lead his team past the Nuggets. Though he would score 34 in Game 4, Kobe and his squad would end up losing Game 4 to a resilient Nuggets team. But that was all the momentum that the Nuggets were able to muster up.

Playing and acting as the decoy in Game 5 after scoring well above 36 points all series long, Kobe Bryant attracted much of the defensive attention to get his other teammates rolling en route to a win. Bryant, with 35 points, six rebounds, and ten assists in Game 6, would be the assassin that struck the killing dagger to the hearts of the Denver Nuggets. The Los Angeles Lakers would win the series and proceed to the NBA Finals for a second consecutive year.

Kobe Bryant and his Los Angeles Lakers would square off with the Orlando Magic in the NBA Finals. Once the opening was tossed, Bryant was in a state of focus unseen before in the history of the NBA. The look in his eyes and the scowl on his face was typical of the Black Mamba that roamed and terrorized the league since 1996. He would strike poisonous jumper after jumper that disheartened and fell the Magic in Game 1. Not even Chris Rock, who was voted the funniest man in America that year, could flinch Kobe with his jokes as he was sitting beside him courtside. Bryant would end the game with 40 points, eight rebounds, and eight assists.

Kobe Bryant would then deliver 29 points and eight assists in Game 2 when the Lakers took a 2-0 advantage in the Finals. Trying to earn the franchise's first ever win in the Finals, the Magic would win Game 3 to survive Bryant's 31 points. But again, Kobe went back to work and finished Orlando off with 62 combined points in Games 4 and 5 to win his first title without Shaquille O'Neal and his first ever Finals MVP award after averaging 32 points.

After winning his fourth NBA title, Bryant would feel relieved and that the monkey was finally off his back. He had dispelled a long-believed notion that he could never win an NBA title without Shaquille O'Neal. However, he did it in spectacular fashion after dominating the Magic defense. He was finally back on top of the basketball world.

Fifth NBA Title

Entering the 2009 offseason, Kobe Bryant was already at the top of the NBA mountain. He was regarded as the best player alongside LeBron James. He was the leading player for a championship team and was the greatest shooting guard of that era. There was nothing left for him to prove since he had already won a title without Shaq. However, Bryant still wanted more. The competitive Mamba in him hungered and craved for more glory.

Realizing he was losing speed and athleticism, Kobe Bryant would find other ways to remain a dominant presence in the NBA. He would seek help from Hakeem Olajuwon, who is regarded as the most fundamentally sound big man in the history of the league. Wanting to learn from the man with thousands of post moves, Bryant flew over to Houston to train with Hakeem. Bryant absorbed all of Olajuwon's teachings and would come into the new season with hundreds of moves added to his already vast offensive repertoire.

With Pau Gasol missing the first 11 games of the season, Kobe Bryant used the absence to show off his improved moves at the low post. Already one of the best guards in NBA history when posting up, Bryant only became better after training with

Hakeem Olajuwon. He would act as the Lakers' primary option at the low post because the triangle offense constantly needs a capable player anchoring the system down low. Bryant would make his defenders pay.

Punishing defenders at the low post, Bryant posted high numbers as Pau Gasol was still recuperating. He would have four games of scoring at least 40 points in the 11-game absence of his 7-foot teammate. And in that span of games, the Lakers held on to their winning ways, only losing three outings. They would only become more dangerous after Pau's return as the Lakers mounted an 11-game winning streak.

And as the Los Angeles Lakers continued to dominate the Western Conference all season long, Kobe Bryant was not short of his patented spectacular clutch moments. He would hit six game-winners that whole season. The first one came on December 4 when he hit an off-balanced one-legged three-point shot off the glass to defeat the Miami Heat. On December 16, Bryant hit the game-winning shot against the Milwaukee Bucks in overtime after missing the one that should have won the Lakers in the fourth quarter. He scored 39 points in that game.

On his way to hitting clutch shot after clutch shot, Kobe Bryant surpassed the 25,000-point mark after scoring 31 points in a loss to the Cleveland Cavaliers on January 21, 2010. He became the youngest player to reach that milestone. Shortly before that, he also hit a clutch three-point shot to win a game against the Sacramento Kings. And, on January 31, he foiled the Boston Celtics by hitting another game-winner in front of the hostile crowd.

After getting named as an All-Star starter despite missing the midseason classic due to injury, Bryant would come back on February 23 to become the cold-blooded Mamba that he was. He hit another game-winner over the Memphis Grizzlies after scoring 32 points on 13 out of 19 shooting the entire game. Then, on March 9, Bryant hit his sixth game-winner of the season versus the Toronto Raptors after scoring 32 points.

At the end of the season, Bryant averaged 27 points, 5.4 rebounds, 5.0 assists, and 1.5 steals despite playing with the same mangled index finger. He would be named to the First Team yet again after also surpassing Jerry West as the franchise's all-time leading scorer. After making six great clutch shots the whole season, Bryant was in full Mamba mode heading into the playoffs.

Once again, the Lakers took first place in the Pacific Division with a record of 57-25, which was good enough to take the first seed in the Western Conference. The 2010 playoffs showed Bryant's dominance once again as he averaged 29.2 points per game throughout the entire tournament while also averaging six rebounds, 5.5 assists, and 1.3 steals per game from the first round against Oklahoma City to the finals against the Boston Celtics.

While the Los Angeles Lakers would face a fierce battle against the young and upstart OKC Thunder in the first round, they would manage to beat them using their experience to their advantage. After facing the tough defense of Thabo Sefolosha in that series, Bryant would only have two great scoring outputs. The first one was in Game 2 when he had 39. The second one was in Game 6 when he finished with 32. In addition to those scoring performances, Bryant also played tight defense against the young OKC guard Russell Westbrook, who he would always compare to a younger version of himself.

In the second round, the LA Lakers would prove their mastery of the Utah Jazz, who they met for the third straight time in the playoffs. Bryant, as he always did, would make minced meat out of the Jazz defense, scoring at least 30 points in that four-game sweep. He would average 32 points in that series against the Utah Jazz.

Though Bryant would take his offensive explosions to the Western Conference Finals against the Phoenix Suns, his team would face a tough battle against a revived offensive attack from their former rivals. Kobe would open the series by posting 40 points on them in a blowout win before finishing Game 2 with 21 points and 13 assists. Despite the double-double efforts put up by Bryant in Games 3 and 4, the Suns would tie the series heading into Game 5.

Game 5 was the turning point of that series. With Kobe Bryant sporting a near triple-double output of 30 points, 11 rebounds, and nine assists, he was tasked with the game-winning shot in the final second of the game. Uncharacteristic of Bryant, who was the most clutch player in the league that season, he would miss the shot. However, Ron Artest came to the rescue by rebounding the shot and putting it back in as time expired to give the Lakers the win. Kobe would then finish the Suns off in Game 6 by posting 37 big points. He would average 33.7 points in that series.

The Lakers met the Celtics in a rematch of the 2008 Finals. It was a tightly-contested series and neither team would give the edge to the other. The Celtics played tight defense on Kobe all series long while the Lakers managed to limit the Big Three's performance despite several three-point explosions from Ray Allen in that series.

It was a back and forth affair. LA would win Game 1 only to lose Game 2. Then, on the strength of Kobe's 29 points, they would lead the series 2-1 only to fall 2-3 after five games heading back to Los Angeles. Kobe was averaging 35.5 points in those last two losses. But the Lakers would blow the Celtics out in Game 6 to make it a series to remember.

This time around, Kobe and the Lakers pulled it off in a classic Game 7 win where they came back from a 13-point deficit in the third quarter. Although Bryant shot just 6 of 24 from the field, he scored 10 points in the fourth quarter in an epic display of willpower and determination. While Kobe was the main catalyst in that comeback, he had to thank Artest for his heroics as the former Defensive Player of the Year was hitting timely shots again. As the dust settled, Bryant finished with 23 points and 15 rebounds to seal his fifth NBA title win and his second Finals MVP award.

Explaining his bad performance in that Game 7 win, Kobe Bryant would say that he just wanted and willed himself to try and win that game because he was so hungry to get back at the Celtics for beating them in 2008. While it was not a good night for him, he would give credit to his teammates for bailing him out of that situation and for giving him his fifth title ring.[ii]

Chapter 8: Chasing MJ

The Fall From the Top

Riding on the high of two straight titles, Bryant started his quest for a sixth title. One of his primary goals was to tie the championships of Michael Jordan, who he was often compared to, especially at that point of his career. At the age of 32, Kobe was more like Michael than he ever was. Both started their careers as athletic beasts that relentlessly attacked the basket. But as they both aged, they relied more on jumpers and post moves to counteract their declining athletic abilities. While Bryant never wanted to be Jordan, there can be no denying how close of a prototype he was to the greatest player of all time.

Meanwhile, Kobe led the Lakers to a great start to the season as he led his team to eight straight victories. One of his highlight performances was when he posted 30 points, ten rebounds, and 12 assists in a win over the Sacramento Kings on November 3. And though it came in a losing effort, he did finish with 41 points on November 28 against the Indiana Pacers.

Because Bryant was putting up consistent scoring numbers all season long despite his age and injuries, the Lakers were on their way to another good regular season record and with a chance of defending their titles. However, they did have a few downsides to their season. The Lakers seemed to have fallen concerning consistency and performance as they were unable to defeat the top four teams in the NBA that season.

Their first win against a top team was when Kobe Bryant scored 20 of his 23 points in the second half of their game against the Boston Celtics on February 10, 2011. Nine days before that game, he became only the seventh player in league history to have a total of 25,000 points, 5,000 rebounds, and 5,000 assists in a career. Another one of his highlights that season was when he scored 37 in the All-Star Game to win the MVP award and tie Bob Pettit in that regard.

It was also during that season when Kobe Bryant started his climb to the top of the NBA's all-time scoring list. On his way to scoring a total of 2,078 points in that season, Bryant would pass the likes of legendary players John Havlicek, Dominque Wilkins, Oscar Robertson, Hakeem Olajuwon, Elvin Hayes, and Moses Malone to become sixth all-time in most points scored in a career. He started the season 12th on that list.

At the end of that difficult season for Kobe Bryant, he would average 25.3 points, 5.1 rebounds, 4.7 assists, and 1.2 steals on his way to another nomination to the All-NBA and All-

Defensive First Teams. He would lead the Lakers to a 57-25 record heading into the playoffs. But despite a good regular season record, there seemed to be something off with the Lakers. They were battling chemistry issues while Bryant was ailing due to a swollen right knee that needed to be drained of fluids from time to time to stop the swelling. That injury may have slowed him down all season long, but Kobe was still the best shooting guard in the league despite the influx of younger and more athletic guards.

As the Los Angeles Lakers marched into the playoffs, the whole world wished for them to regain their championship form in the hopes of having them reach the NBA Finals to face the newly formed super team of the Miami Heat composed of LeBron James, Dwyane Wade, and Chris Bosh. However, the Lakers never regained their best form and struggled against lower-seeded opponents.

The Lakers would find it difficult to beat the New Orleans Hornets in the first round of the playoffs and were pushed to six games. Uncharacteristic of Kobe was how he struggled to shoot from the floor. In those six games, he would only score above 20 points three times. What was even worse was his performance against the Dallas Mavericks in the second round. Bryant would never come close to the 36 points he put up in

Game 1 while the Mavericks pounded them all series long for a four-game sweep of the two-time defending champions.

The Mamba Becoming Vino

After that disappointing exit in the playoffs for the former two-time defending champions, Kobe Bryant decided knew that it was his injuries that slowed his team down considering he was always the cog that had kept the Los Angeles Lakers going for nearly a decade and a half. Bryant would go to Germany for an experimental procedure to fix the ailment in his right knee.

Bryant's trip to Germany was a success. The treatment he involved doctors draining him of platelet-rich blood, which was manipulated and re-introduced to the body, particularly in the ailing part, to relieve inflammation and chronic pain. While it the procedure seemed simple and a little macabre, Kobe Bryant's knee returned to its full healthy form as the Black Mamba got back to the state that won him the MVP during the 2008 season.

Unfortunately for Kobe Bryant, his beloved coach, Phil Jackson, who used to be one of his biggest critics and detractors, decided to call his coaching career quits and would not return to coach the Lakers. Replacing him was Mike Brown, who was made famous in Cleveland by the brilliant seasons that the Cavaliers had under the leadership of LeBron James. Brown, known for relying on superstars, would put all of his hopes on the 33-year-old Kobe Bryant.

Kobe would not let his new coach down. The man that critics had once called too old and worn down was putting up great overall numbers, especially on the scoring end. Early in January of that lockout-shortened season, Bryant would pile up four consecutive games of scoring 40 or more points. It started when he had 48 points against the Phoenix Suns before putting up 40, 42, and 42 against the Jazz, Cavs, and the Clippers. Because of his performances at such an advanced age in basketball years, Bryant gained a new nickname—Vino. He was like a fine wine getting better with age.

As the All-Star Game came, Bryant was out there to chase Michael Jordan and history once more when he scored 27 points and moved past the great one to become the all-time leader in points scored in the midseason classic. However, Bryant would break his nose in that game when Wade fouled him. Because of that, Kobe would wear an infamous black mask while his nose was healing.

Wearing that black mask and showing no signs of slowing down, Kobe would score 30 or more points in three consecutive games, which were all wins for the Lakers. In the meantime, the Los Angeles Lakers were playing well under Brown as Bryant, Gasol, and Bynum were three All-Stars leading the team in that transition season.

Early in April, Bryant would score 40 points for the final time that season. Shortly after that, he would miss seven games in April due to a bruised left shin. Bryant would return with only three games remaining on their schedule, and he had a chance to win his third scoring title had he chosen to. He was second all season long to Durant in scoring, but ceded the title to the younger star as Kobe was mature enough not to let his personal goals get between his desire to win.

As he planned, Kobe Bryant would finish the season as the second-leading scorer in the league. He averaged an incredible stat line of 27.9 points, 5.4 rebounds, and 4.6 assists for a 33-year old veteran. He was named to the All-NBA First Team and the All-Defensive Second Team. That was the last time he would be named to an All-Defensive Team as he held a record of 12 selections in that regard.

Playoff bound once more, the Lakers would face a tough battle in the first round against the Denver Nuggets, who pushed them to seven games. Despite the struggle to get past the Nuggets,

Bryant had several great scoring performances in that series. He had 31 and 38 points in Games 1 and 2, which were both wins. In a losing effort in Game 5, he had 43 points before putting up 31 in another loss in Game 6. His Lakers, however, would beat the Nuggets in Game 7 to proceed to the second round.

Against the title favorite Thunder team, the Lakers would only win a single game in five tries as the younger OKC squad clobbered them. After scoring only 40 combined points in Games 1 and 2 of that series, Kobe scored 36 in Game 3, which was their lone win. He then had 38 and 42 points as he tried to punish the Thunder all by himself. However, the Thunder proved to be fresher and hungrier, defeating the Lakers in five games. That was the final playoff run for the five-time champion Kobe Bryant.

Chapter 9: The Injury Years and Retirement

The Achilles Tear that Shattered a Career

After that loss to the OKC Thunder in the second round of the 2012 playoffs, the Lakers realized they needed to revamp their roster to keep up with the demands of an increasingly competitive landscape. Other teams had resorted to having superstars join forces on the same roster to dominate the field.

With that, the Los Angeles Lakers acquired Dwight Howard in a trade that centered around Andrew Bynum. They also traded for the old but still reliable point guard, Steve Nash, who always wanted to play for LA. Because of the additions of two key pieces, the Lakers were suddenly favorites again as Kobe Bryant was about to lead a pack of current and former All-Stars in the form of Dwight Howard, Pau Gasol, Steve Nash, and Metta World Peace (formerly Ron Artest).

Because of the addition of the new pieces, coach Mike Brown would implement a new scheme called the Princeton Offense. Unfortunately, the experiment would not work because the system failed to utilize the formidable talent that the Lakers had. The failed experiment also led to Brown's firing.

But before Brown was fired, Kobe had one of the most memorable moments caught on camera. Brown passed by Bryant as he sat on the bench in one of the Lakers' early games that season. As soon as Brown walked past, Kobe gazed at him with an angry look in his eyes. That look would be dubbed as the infamous Kobe "death stare."

With the influence of Kobe Bryant, the Lakers would hire former Phoenix Suns head coach Mike D'Antoni instead of offering Phil Jackson a huge contract to come back and coach one of the most talented teams ever assembled in franchise history. However, even D'Antoni was not equipped with enough skills to steer the sinking ship into the right direction.

Steve Nash was out the majority of that season with back ailments. Pau Gasol was being underutilized by the coach and was primarily placed on the perimeter as a jump shooter instead of the low post threat he truly was. Despite still playing like an All-Star, Dwight Howard was not his full beastly self and struggled with the pressure of being in LA. He feuded with Bryant about who was the true alpha dog on the Laker roster, but Kobe never feuded with Howard because of ego. He just did not like how the big man lacked the competitive spirit needed to win titles.

Because of those factors and several others, the Los Angeles Lakers struggled all season long to stay on their feet and above the 50% mark concerning wins. But behind all those struggles was the 34-year-old Kobe Bryant, who was still playing like the superstar he truly was. Indeed, he was like a fine wine that only got better and better with age. Bryant mastered his jump shot and punished defenders with his fundamental skills, primarily at the post. Kobe was the only bright spot for the Lakers that season.

Kobe had a lot of highlight performances at an advanced basketball age. During December, he mounted together what would become a 10-game streak of scoring at least 30 or more points. He had two 40-point games during that streak. And with Nash injured, Bryant also became the team's primary playmaker because D'Antoni's system needed a good point guard to become active. Kobe would have several highlight assists games including three straight outings with at least 11 dimes. He had back-to-back 14-assist games in that span late in January 2013.

In line with another All-Star start for Bryant, the legendary Laker would then have 40 points against the Portland Trail Blazers shortly after the midseason break. After that game, he had 38 against the Mavs on February 24. Both games were wins.

Then, on March 6 and 8, Bryant displayed his mastery as a scorer and facilitator when he had consecutive 40-10 double-doubles on points and assists. He had 42 points and 12 dimes against the Hornets before beating the Raptors with 41 markers and 12 assists.

Nearly a month after those great back-to-back performances, Kobe Bryant would become the first player in league history to have 47 points, eight rebounds, five assists, three steals, and four blocks in a single game. That happened on April 10 against the Portland Trail Blazers. He did that at the age of 34. Black Mamba, Vino, or whatever you call him, Kobe Bryant's skills were like no other. Not even the younger players could duplicate what he could do.

However, tragedy was quick to strike its hand upon the streaking hot Kobe Bryant, who was on the cusp of yet another All-Star appearance. Right after his memorable performance against the Blazers, he would score 34 points against the Golden State Warriors. But near the end of the game, he drove on the Warriors' Harrison Barnes and suddenly felt a pop in his right Achilles. He would wince in pain before walking off the court on his own two feet.

When diagnosed, it was revealed that Kobe Bryant had suffered a tear in his right Achilles tendon. He would have surgery on April 13 and would miss the remainder of the season after averaging 27.3 points, 5.6 rebounds, 6.0 assists, and 1.4 steals. The last time a 34-year-old averaged those kinds of numbers was when Jordan was winning MVP's back in the mid-90s. That was how great Kobe was that season as he would watch his Lakers crumble in the first round of the playoffs.

The injury would frustrate Bryant to the fullest. He said that he had made the same move a million times in the past, but he had never got injured because of it. He was frustrated because after conquering dozens of obstacles in his career, another mountain stood in the way of his quest for greatness.[ii] It was going to be another long healing process for Kobe Bryant, whose great career ended on the night he tore his tendon.

The Six-Game Season, the Fractured Knee

Kobe Bryant would promptly begin rehabbing the torn tendon after it healed post-surgery. But Kobe would never even get on the court to practice with the Lakers until November 2013. Bryant spent a very long time rehabbing and trying to strengthen that part of his body again to prepare his 35-year-old physique for the grind of another NBA season.

Shortly after returning to practice, the Lakers would tender a two-year extension to Bryant. It was reportedly worth nearly $50 million. Though the contract extension was not without criticism because the large sum that Bryant was getting with would prevent the team from doing major free agent signings and acquisitions, Kobe was worth every penny for the blood, sweat, and tears he had shed for the Lakers since 1996.

Bryant would make his much-awaited return on December 10, 2013, against the Phoenix Suns. By that time, the Lakers were a whole new team. Nash was still injured, and Howard was off playing in Houston. The only familiar face was Pau Gasol, who still dreaded playing under Mike D'Antoni as he felt his skills were underappreciated.

For Kobe's part, he forced himself to become relevant again, scoring 20 points in his return game. However, he would only combine for a total of 54 points in the next five games. Something was off. Bryant was still struggling to get back to peak form. The Lakers would suddenly sideline Kobe as he was suffering from a fractured knee. Whether the injury was an accident or brought about by the increased pressure due to the injured Achilles tendon, one thing was clear: Kobe Bryant's body was beginning to break down. He would not return that season despite getting named as a starter for the Western All-

Stars. Feeling he did not deserve the selection, Bryant would not play in that game.

Complete Body Breakdown, Kobe Trying to Defy Father Time

Kobe Bryant, entering his 19th season in the NBA as a 36-year old, would return to action for the LA Lakers just in time for the opening game of the 2014-15 season. At that moment, everybody thought that Kobe had broken through all the obstacles that had plagued his body for the past two seasons. They were thinking that Bryant had achieved the impossible in trying to defy the effects of wear and tear on his way to another Mamba-like season.

Trying to get back to top superstar form quickly, Bryant would shoot his way to great scoring performances. He had 31 in his second game back and 39 in his fifth. He would even score 44 points on the Golden State Warriors on November 16. However, all those performances came at losses. Bryant was also so inefficient when trying to score his way out of his struggles because his shooting clips were well below his average. Moreover, his scoring performances were far too few in between mediocre and poor outputs.

However, despite the fact that he and his team were struggling, Kobe Bryant would have 31 points, 11 rebounds, and 12 assists in a win over the Toronto Raptors on November 30 to become the oldest player with at least 30 points in a triple-double effort. In his next game, he then had 13 assists as the Mamba was trying to get his unfamiliar and young teammates going. And on December 14, Kobe Bryant officially passed Michael Jordan to become third all-time in most points scored in a career.

However, those were the only few highlights that Bryant could muster up that season as a combination of injuries plagued him. Bryant's shoulder, knees, and Achilles tendon continued to bother him throughout that season. The global superstar's body just could not keep up with the skill level he had been displaying on the hard court. He would undergo season-ending surgery to fix all his ailments, but not before dishing out a high of 17 assists in a loss to the Cleveland Cavaliers on January 15, 2015.

In that weak attempt of a comeback season, Kobe Bryant would only play in 35 games for the Los Angeles Lakers. He would average 22.3 points, 5.7 rebounds, and 5.6 assists while playing nearly 35 minutes a night. The worse part was that he was shooting only 37.4% from the floor to mark the first ever season where he shot below 40%. His Lakers, undergoing a rebuilding period, would end up with one of the worst records in the NBA that season.

The Retirement Tour

Kobe Bryant would be cleared to play for the 2015-16 season since he had fully recovered from the injuries that ailed him that past season. However, the biggest question that if he could get back to at least half of his superstar form now that he was entering the season as a 37-year-old in his 20th year for the Lakers. Kobe had officially passed John Stockton's record of 19 seasons in one franchise.

No matter how much he tried, Bryant would never get back to his top form or even a quarter of it as his body had completely refused to cooperate with his skill level and mental toughness. Kobe would hover below 20 points a game for the majority of the season as good scoring nights from him became a rarity. The best he could come up with early on was his 31-point output in a win over the Washington Wizards. That performance came three days after he had decided to call it a career.

On November 29, 2015, Kobe Bryant, through the Player's Tribune, wrote a letter to the game of basketball explaining his plans of retiring and leaving at the end of the season. "My mind can handle the grind, but my body knows it's time to say goodbye," were Bryant's exact words as he bid farewell to basketball, his first and only true love. After that announcement, the whole Laker season and probably the entire year of the NBA was dedicated to Kobe Bryant in what would become his retirement tour.

Realizing they would never see the greatness of Kobe Bryant ever again, opposing teams and arenas welcomed Kobe Bryant with open arms and with cheers louder than what they could muster up for their home teams. Always hated by many other cities for the way he killed their teams, Bryant's legend earned him the great reverence and respect by even the most rabid fanbases.

As a testament to his popularity and undying support from the fans, Kobe Bryant was voted to the All-Star team as the starter that garnered nearly 2 million votes more than the second highest vote-getter. Like many other games that Kobe played that season, the 2016 All-Star Game became a sendoff party for the 18-time All-Star. Bryant would score 10 points in nearly 26 minutes in his final appearance in the midseason classic.

Later on, Kobe Bryant would end his remarkable and legendary career in the best of ways—by scoring. In what was the Lakers' final game that season, Bryant prepared himself for a possible grind. His team fought back from a deficit against the Utah Jazz, who respected Bryant all game long. Kobe was getting shots up the whole game as he led the Lakers back from the deficit by endlessly putting up attempt after attempt. On a jumper, Bryant would give the Lakers the lead for good before ending his career with his final play—an assist. At the end of what was an exhausting game for Kobe Bryant, the Mamba finished with 60 points on 50 shots from the field and a win to boot. It was the best way to go for such a dominant scorer as Kobe Bryant.

As Kobe Bryant faded quietly into the night throughout the season, words from personalities, players, friends, coaches, and legends began to surface as they bid their farewells and parting words to the legendary Laker guard. With all those words said, nothing meant more to Kobe than the final words that basketball uttered for him—a silent swoosh through the hoop when he made his last shot in the NBA.

Post-Retirement

After retiring, Kobe Bryant has not made a lot of plans for his future other than spending more time with his wife and kids after dedicating his whole life to basketball. However, Bryant did express his desire of getting into venture investment as an entrepreneur.

Bryant would form a partnership with Jeff Stibel, the former CEO of Web.com, to launch an investment fund they called Bryant Stibel. The focus of the investment would center on technology and media as Bryant would say that he wanted to leave a lasting impact outside of the game of basketball by inspiring the next generation in the realm of data.[xii]

Chapter 10: International Dominance

In his time in the NBA, Bryant has won five separate league championships with the Los Angeles Lakers with several awards and accomplishments, including two NBA Finals MVP awards and 17 selections to the annual All-Star Game. But he also has a few gold medals while wearing the red, white and blue uniform of the United States men's basketball team during multiple international competitions.

There were a lot of changes to the roster when looking back to the 2004 US Olympic basketball team when America had to settle for only the bronze medal in the games held in Athens, Greece. They struggled to qualify for the medal round of the competition with the last berth from Group B after finishing 3-2 in pool play and losing to Argentina 89-81 in the semifinals. Argentina would win the gold medal while the USA had to be okay with facing Lithuania – barely defeating them, 104-96. It was only the third time in Olympic history where the United States was unable to win the gold medal and the first since they began enlisting NBA players to the team.

Changes were then made throughout the entire USA Basketball operations, starting with making Jerry Colangelo the person who would select the team's roster for future international tournaments. Players who would be chosen were told that they need to commit for at least three years at a time to help establish a more centered team. But in the 2006 FIBA World Championship, the United States was eliminated by Greece during the semifinal game 101-95 despite Carmelo Anthony leading the team with nearly 20 points per game. The team would then make the coaching changes with new head coach Mike Krzyzewski – known for his time at Duke University – and an assistant coaching staff that included Jim Boeheim (Syracuse University), Mike D'Antoni (Phoenix Suns) and Nate McMillan (Portland Trail Blazers).

Additions were made to USA Basketball to include players like Bryant and the players mentioned who were part of the team that competed at the 2008 Summer Olympics. But in a tune-up tournament, the USA was able to sweep the entire competition during the 2007 FIBA Tournament of the Americas Championship. This was highlighted by Bryant scoring 31 points in the team's 118-81 victory over Argentina on September 2, 2007. However, Bryant's first Olympic appearance was at the 2008 Summer Olympics in Beijing, China. He was part of a team that was more like an All-Star team of many star NBA players that included Dwayne Wade, LeBron James, Dwight Howard, and Chris Bosh.

Because there was so much star power, each of the stars was taking turns as the leading scorer for each of the five games in pool play with the USA going 5-0. It started with a 101-70 victory over the host country China on August 10, 2008, where Wade had 19 points, followed by James with 18 points, while Bryant had 13 points with two rebounds, three assists, and two steals. Bryant was also given a little bit of rest as he had eight points and four rebounds in the United States' 97-76 win over Angola two days later. Bryant had 18 points to share the top scoring lead with Bosh in a 92-69 win over Greece on August 14, 2008.

Bryant had 11 and 13 points respectively as the USA would sweep the entire Group B with a 119-82 win over Spain (August 16, 2008) and Germany 106-57 (August 18, 2008). His numbers may seem pretty average compared to what he had been putting up with the Lakers. But then again, he was sharing the ball with some highly talented athletes on a team that featured a collection of players that could have given Michael Jordan's "Dream Team" a run for its money. Bryant would have a few breakout games in the 2008 Summer Olympics, including the quarterfinals victory where the United States defeated Australia 116-85 on August 20, 2008. This win was credited mainly to Bryant's overall leading 25 points and five rebounds with an assist, a steal, and a block. It is worth noting that James nearly had a double-double with 16 points and nine rebounds in that win as well. Bryant would then score another 12 points in the team's 101-81 victory in the semifinal round on August 22, 2008.

Bryant was a key contributor in the United States' gold-medal win with 20 points, six assists, and three rebounds in the team's 118-107 victory over Spain. Also helping Bryant bring America the gold medal was Wade's 27 points and James' 14 points and six rebounds.

Four years later, Bryant returned to USA Basketball as part of a team that looked to defend their gold medal at the 2012 Summer Olympics in London, England. Bryant was once again one of several NBA stars that would create their version of the "Dream Team." With other returning stars like Anthony and James, there was plenty of new blood joining the team like Kevin Durant, Kevin Love, Russell Westbrook, and Chris Paul. With so much talent on the team, it was one of the few times where Bryant would score only 10 points and still have his team win – like in the 98-71 victory over France on July 29, 2012, the first of their 5-0 run in Group A action.

After the United States had defeated Tunisia 110-63 – a game where Bryant played only nine minutes with four points – he was one of six players to score in double digits in the team's 156-73 win over Nigeria on August 2, 2012. Bryant had 16 points, three rebounds, two assists, and two steals in only 11 minutes. Anthony led the team with 37 points, followed by Westbrook's 21 points. The USA would then face a tough test against Lithuania where they were able to hold off the upset 99-94 on August 4, 2012, in a game where Bryant got six points over 20 minutes. Bryant also had 11 points in 21 minutes to help the United States defeat Argentina 126-97. While he did not act as a top contributor to Team USA, he would become a key factor in the medal round with 20 points during the team's 119-86 win on August 8, 2012. Bryant would score most of his points from beyond the three-point arc, going 6 out of 10 with three assists and two steals.

Bryant would have another 13 points with 50 percent shooting from the field in the team's semifinal 109-83 win over Argentina on August 10, 2012. That game also featured four other players scoring in double digits, including 19 points from Durant, 18 points from both Anthony and James, and Paul's 10 points. But Durant started to show that he was becoming one of the key young players for the US men's basketball team as he would score 30 points in 38 minutes to help the Americans defeat Spain 107-100 in the gold-medal match on August 12, 2012. Bryant still made plays with 17 points with a few rebounds, assists, and a steal.

Bryant's two gold medals match the number that Jordan has (1984, 1992). One would believe that Bryant would want to take a break from wearing the American colors in international play as he reaches the age of 36. Likewise, who knows how many more years he will be willing to play professionally? The 2015-2016 season will be Bryant's 19th season with the Los Angeles Lakers after dealing with injuries for the past two years.

But in an August article in the Los Angeles Times from Ben Bolch, Bryant revealed that he may not be finished with Team USA. In what might be a sign of the fact that Bryant is thinking about retirement, USA Basketball chairman of player selection Jerry Colangelo revealed to media members that Bryant wants to have one last run for the gold medal at the 2016 Summer Olympics that will be held in Rio de Janeiro. He even used the old phrase "ride out into the sunset." However, that does not mean that Bryant is just going to walk onto the team in time to make the trip to South America. He will have to earn his spot on the roster, just like all of the other NBA players who have been invited to the upcoming trial camp, and that is seemingly going to be perfect for the very competitive Bryant.

There are some concerns as he is getting closer to the age of 37 years old and has not been 100 percent healthy with the Lakers. However, he is expected to be ready for a full season starting in 2016 after playing in only 41 games in the previous two seasons. This sort of thinking has some controversy. Some have felt that Bryant earning a spot on Team USA will be another achievement to add to his already impressive list of accomplishments. There are others on the other side of the fence who feel that Bryant would actually take a spot away from someone who is in their prime and could eventually be a negative roster move.

The final decisions will be made by both Colangelo and head coach Krzyzewski at some point in 2016 before the beginning of the Olympic training camp in the early summer months. There is also the concern when it comes to his health from the last few seasons. But it will be interesting to see how well he does in the 2015-16 season, and that could help build up to what could be another run for an Olympic gold and a chance to have more gold medals than most NBA stars – including Jordan.

Chapter 11: Bryant's Personal Life

Even before he took Los Angeles by storm, life was already Hollywood-like for the young Kobe Bryant. After a magical high school basketball career, he ended that part of his life in style by taking Grammy award winning singer Brandy to Lower Merion High's prom as his date.

The 17-year-old High School basketball phenomenon and TV star/singer met while he was in New York for the Essence Awards. Brandy did not attend the award show, but she was in New York, too. So when Kobe told his friend Mike Harris, who owned a sports management firm together with Boyz II Men member Michael McCary, that he admired Brandy, Harris hooked the two young stars up. After Bryant popped the prom question and Brandy said "yes," the two spent the night before the event in Atlantic City to watch Barry White perform.

When the young couple arrived at the Bellevue in Center City where the prom was held, they were mobbed by a crowd of paparazzi and curious onlookers. Kobe Bryant had his first episode of being in the spotlight during a social occasion, while for Brandy Norwood it was just another day at the office.

Kobe later said that he and Brandy had their private moments when they were inside the venue. But even there, Kobe's classmates and fellow seniors were awed by the star power of the couple that the cameras kept clicking all night long with students and parents taking turns to have their photo taken with the couple. They were both just teenagers back then, but that glimpse of a Hollywood life was just the beginning for Kobe Bryant.

As Bryant became an NBA star, the other facets of Hollywood started opening up for him. One of those areas was music. In 1999, Bryant tried to venture into the rap business as an artist. On one occasion while filming a rap video, Kobe Bryant met Vanessa Laine. Vanessa was a 17-year-old high school senior at the Marina High School in Huntington Beach, California. She was an aspiring model and was working in the same studio at that time as a background dancer for a Snoop Dogg video. Although the music video and debut rap album that Kobe recorded was never released, he and Vanessa became an instant hit.

After just six months of dating, their whirlwind romance led to an engagement in May of 2000. When Kobe popped the question, he gave his future wife a 7-carat, $100K engagement ring. One month later, Kobe got another all-important ring: his first ever NBA championship ring.

On April 18, 2001, Lakers' superstar Kobe Bryant, at only 22 years of age, married 18-year-old Vanessa Laine at the St. Edward the Confessor Catholic Church in Dana Point, California, which was some 90 minutes south of LA. In contrast to Bryant's hard court flare, the couple chose a rare day off for the Lakers' star to insert the surprise wedding, which was attended by only 12 people. Not one of Kobe's parents or his two sisters were present during the marriage; not even his long-time adviser, Arn Tellem. Even Kobe's teammates knew of the wedding only during the team practice the following day. And instead of going on a honeymoon after the wedding, Vanessa watched her new husband four days later play 41 minutes and drop 28 points on the Portland Trail Blazers in a winning performance during Game 1 of their 2001 Western Conference first-round playoff series.

But the wedding became controversial because it caused a rift between Kobe Bryant and his family. That estrangement lasted for more than two years, and Kobe never had contact with any member of his family during that period. According to Kobe himself via The Times in 2003, his parents were uncomfortable because Kobe's bride was "Latina" and not "African-American." He went on to add that his father, Joe, was not happy about Kobe's "utter devotion" to Vanessa. There were also reports that his family objected to the marriage because Vanessa was only 18 at the time.

On January 19, 2003, Vanessa Bryant gave birth to their first born, Natalia Diamante. Upon the request of Vanessa, Kobe slowly patched things up with his family. By the time Joe Bryant was named coach of the LA Sparks in 2005, the Bryant family looked like one solid team once again.

After an ectopic pregnancy caused a miscarriage in 2005, Vanessa gave birth to their second daughter, Gianna Maria-Onor'e, on May 1, 2006, six minutes ahead of the birth of Shaquille O'Neal's daughter, Me'arah Sanaa. But before Gianna was born, she almost was not conceived in the first place as the marriage was nearly blown apart by a serious controversy.

In 2003, Kobe Bryant was arrested by police officers from the sheriff's office in Eagle, Colorado following a sexual assault case filed by a 19-year-old female employee of a Colorado hotel called The Lodge and Spa at Cordillera. The woman claimed that Bryant raped her in his hotel room on July 1, the night before Bryant had a scheduled knee surgery with famed specialist Dr. Richard Steadman. Bryant denied the allegations of an assault but admitted to having consensual sex with his accuser.

On July 18, the Eagle County District Attorney's Office formally charged Bryant with one count of sexual assault, and it seemed that the NBA's biggest star had fallen from grace. But as resilient as ever, Bryant held a press conference on the same day he was charged, and he vehemently denied raping the woman. He, however, tearfully admitted to having an adulterous sexual encounter with her.

Vanessa sat beside her husband during that press conference to show the world that she was standing by her man. However, she was criticized for sitting beside Kobe while he was admitting an adulterous sexual encounter and for receiving an 8-carat purple diamond ring worth around $4 million from her philandering spouse. But no, Vanessa did not condone Kobe's act and said he was wrong. However, she had to be strong and fight for the family that they both had fought for right from the very beginning.

With his woman behind him all the way, Kobe Bryant and his Dream Team of lawyers fought the battle and salvaged what was left of the image that Bryant had established in seven seasons with the Lakers.

Bryant had cultivated a clean image in the NBA. He was idolized by millions of kids all over the world because of his charm and otherworldly basketball gifts. His Lakers were sitting on top of the NBA world after winning three consecutive NBA titles while his family had just added their first little girl six months before the incident. Kobe lost millions in endorsement deals with McDonalds and Nutella, among others. Despite the money lost, it was far from the damage that his image took. Everything seemed to fall apart in a single accusation that was never proved in court.

The hearings began, and uglier details of the incident came out. It was not just Kobe's character that was under attack and scrutiny. His lawyers tried their best to do the same to his accuser. Finally, on September 1, 2004, the charges against Kobe Bryant were dropped after the woman declined to testify in court.

Aside from the criminal case, a civil case was also filed against Bryant. But with the heavier criminal liability now gone, Bryant settled the civil case out of court. Although the exact details of the settlement were not disclosed, it involved a public apology which Bryant made to the woman, her family, and Eagle, Colorado.

Looking back, Kobe said that period was tough for him and his family. He admitted that there were days that seemed endless and he used to feel it was not going to end. However, in those darkest moments, he turned back to the escape that made him who he was: basketball.

Although he heard occasional boos and jeers when he entered the basketball court, especially in Denver, Kobe Bryant's NBA career flourished after that incident. He was able to win his only MVP in 2008 and led the Lakers to two more NBA titles in 2009 and 2010. Unfortunately, while everything was rebounding perfectly well inside the court, his personal life was starting to fall apart once again.

After ten years of marriage and a dropped sex assault charge, Vanessa Bryant filed for divorce citing "irreconcilable differences." One year later, Vanessa became a regular at the Lakers' games once again, and the couple officially reconciled and said that they were moving on with their lives as a family.

Chapter 12: Impact on Basketball

Kobe Bryant has always been synonymous with work ethic and commitment. First of all, his attitude towards both is indeed incredible. His dedication to his craft is unparalleled in this generation.

Bryant has always been compared to Michael Jordan. And if there is one person who could say who is better, it is New York Knicks President Phil Jackson, who coached Kobe to five titles and Jordan to six titles. When pressed about the comparison, Jackson gave Bryant the nod in one important aspect of the game: dedication to training.

A story on reddit.com by an athletic trainer named "Robert" tells just how crazy Kobe Bryant is about training. The story supposedly happened during Team USA's preparations for the 2012 London Olympics. Kobe Bryant reportedly called the trainer at 3:15 a.m. and asked if he could help him out with some conditioning work. When the trainer obliged, he was surprised to see Kobe Bryant drenched in sweat as if he had been playing for hours even though it was not even 5 a.m. yet. After they were done with the short conditioning session, the trainer went back to bed and returned during his 11:00 a.m. call. He saw Kobe by his lonesome, shooting hoops on one side of the facility. As they talked, he asked Bryant what time he finished his shooting drills earlier that morning. Bryant's reply was "just now." Rob learned that Kobe wanted to shoot 800 makes before calling it a day.

That was just one of the many stories about Kobe Bryant's dedication to training and his never-ending effort to better himself as a player. The thing with Bryant is that he has never failed to push himself harder, not even when he is this "old."

When Bryant went down with a season-ending knee injury last December, he could not just sit on his two-year $48 million contract extension and wait for things to come to him. Instead, Bryant came up to the media around the 2014 All-Star break and demanded that the Lakers surround him with pieces because he wants a win before he retires.

The Lakers already hinted that they were planning to splurge on free agents in 2016 as Kevin Durant would become a free agent, however, with Kobe's demand for a "win now" season, the Lakers made a bid for Carmelo Anthony and LeBron James in the offseason. When that did not happen, they picked up Jeremy Lin and Carlos Boozer to help Kobe this coming 2015 season.

The Lakers do not seem to have a line-up that could finish among the Top 8 in the Western Conference in 2015. It is

Bryant's resilience and indomitable will that will be a spectacle to behold and something every other player must have.

Even when he was in high school, Kobe was the personification of hard work and commitment. He was the kid who took the extra hours at the gym after practices, despite the fact that he was already the best there was. When a lot of teams passed on him in the '96 draft, he just worked and worked harder until he finally got to the summit.

Kevin Garnett broke the long silence of "Prep-to-Pro" players in 1995, but Kobe Bryant asserted that right the following year by becoming the first ever guard to be selected straight from high school. Bryant was only the 6th high school player to be drafted in the NBA. After Kobe Bryant in 1996, 36 more high school superstars went straight to the NBA until the one and done rule was implemented by the NBA in 2003. At least 21 of those 36 prep stars are still playing in the NBA today. LeBron James is the most notable.

In short, names like Darryl Dawkins and Kevin Garnett opened the doors, but it was Kobe Bryant who paved the way for the high school stars to take a leap of fate and go straight to the NBA.

Other than paving the way for high school players that made the jump to the NBA, one of Kobe Bryant's lasting impacts to the game on basketball was, of course, his whole evolution. Bryant came into the league as an athletic teenager full of promise and potential, but was very arrogant and egotistical. Over the years, he refined his body, skills, and talents to become a deadly force from all over the floor whether it was outside the three-point line, in the perimeter, or down at the low post. And, above all that, Bryant matured into the perfect leader and role model for any aspiring basketball star to follow.

Chapter 13: Kobe Bryant's Legacy and Future

Even when Bryant entered the NBA, his doubters did not diminish. When his first couple of seasons in the NBA did not go as well as expected, those detractors grew in number. Even when he started to win titles, his critics said that he was imitating Michael Jordan, that he could not win titles without Shaquille O'Neal, and that he was too selfish of a player to become a team leader.

It is no secret that Kobe watched Michael Jordan's moves while perfecting his repertoire. Kobe has never denied that, and Michael Jordan has always reminded us of that. In fact, the similarities in their moves are striking. Bryant has Jordan's hang time, the unstoppable turnaround jumper, the pull-up shot from a crossover and yes, Kobe's been sticking out his tongue in some of his gravity-defying moves. Still, these similarities do not make Kobe an MJ clone at best.

Jordan called it the evolution of basketball. His Airness said he would not have been who he was without watching David Thompson play, just as Bryant would not have been Kobe Bryant if he did not watch Michael Jordan. When Jordan was interviewed during the launch of the video game NBA 2K14, he said that if there was any player out there who could beat him one-on-one, it was Kobe Bryant. The reason he gave was that Kobe Bryant stole his moves.

But the similarities between Michael Jordan and Kobe Bryant go beyond the moves. These two NBA greats have been compared by titles won and individual achievements. While his critics say his accomplishments pale in comparison to Michael Jordan, Kobe Bryant can say that he has toppled Mike in one aspect—the All-Time Scoring List.

But even though Kobe Bryant has reached the pinnacle of success by finishing third in that list above his idol and his greatest inspiration, Bryant himself became the hero and inspiration. He has instilled the same tenacity, hard work, mental toughness, and competitiveness in many of today's generation's younger NBA players. While Bryant and many of his peers watched and idolized Jordan in their journey to the NBA, today's generation of players wanted to be Kobe Bryant.

Russell Westbrook, a guard playing for the Oklahoma City Thunder, had always loved and admired Kobe's competitive fire and tenacity for basketball. Westbrook has displayed those same qualities time and time again in his quest for personal greatness as he used Bryant as an inspirational figure. He also was a hardheaded kid that was all potential at first. Russ would later mold himself through hard work and dedication into one of the most feared superstars in the NBA.

While Cleveland Cavaliers point guard Kyrie Irving might not have the same ferocious look and intensity that Kobe Bryant displayed in his younger years, he resembles the calmer, decisive, and calculating Kobe Bryant in his older prime years. Irving grew up idolizing Kobe Bryant and has grown to be so competitive to the point of challenging the Mamba himself to a one-on-one game during a Team USA practice. And in Game 7 of the 2016 NBA Finals, Kyrie Irving hit the game-winning three-pointer with only one thing in his mind—Mamba Mentality.

But probably nobody else in the league idolized Kobe Bryant more than Pacers forward Paul George. George would personally admit that he grew up wanting to be Kobe so much that he had all the Laker guard's gear, posters, souvenirs, and memorabilia in his home when he was a teenager. In his younger years, he would even try to emulate Bryant's mannerisms, scowl, and moves while also donning the number 24 when he first started in the NBA. After rising to stardom, George has since carved his identity while changing his number to 13. Nevertheless, he still idolizes Bryant so much.

Many players, fans, and coaches would say different views and opinions about Bryant's legacy to the game of basketball. Some would say that he was the best Michael Jordan clone ever to walk the earth. Others would claim that his effort, undying dedication, and love for the game of basketball were his lasting imprint to the next generation. And some would raise the point that his Mamba Mentality was his greatest gift to basketball.

Despite those many views and opinions, the world would not argue the belief that all of Bryant's 20 seasons, 18-All Star appearances, five NBA titles, and 33,643 points lead to one conclusion. Kobe Bryant's greatest legacy to the next generation and best impact on the game of basketball was, of course, himself.

Final Word/About the Author

I was born and raised in Norwalk, Connecticut. Growing up, I could often be found spending many nights watching basketball, soccer, and football matches with my father in the family living room. I love sports and everything that sports can embody. I believe that sports are one of most genuine forms of competition, heart, and determination. I write my works to learn more about influential athletes in the hopes that from my writing, you the reader can walk away inspired to put in an equal if not greater amount of hard work and perseverance to pursue your goals. If you enjoyed *Kobe Bryant: The Inspiring Story of One of Basketball's Greatest Shooting Guards,* please leave a review! Also, you can read more of my works on *Rob Gronkowski, Brett Favre, Calvin Johnson, Drew Brees, J.J. Watt, Colin Kaepernick, Aaron Rodgers, Peyton Manning, Tom Brady, Russell Wilson, Michael Jordan, LeBron James, Kyrie Irving, Klay Thompson, Stephen Curry, Kevin Durant, Russell Westbrook, Anthony Davis, Chris Paul, Blake Griffin, Joakim Noah, Scottie Pippen, Carmelo Anthony, Kevin Love, Grant Hill, Tracy McGrady, Vince Carter, Patrick Ewing, Karl Malone, Tony Parker, Allen Iverson, Hakeem Olajuwon, Reggie Miller, Michael Carter-Williams, John Wall, James Harden, Tim Duncan, Steve Nash, Draymond Green, Kawhi Leonard,*

Dwyane Wade, Ray Allen, Pau Gasol, Dirk Nowitzki, Jimmy Butler, Paul Pierce, Manu Ginobili, Pete Maravich, Larry Bird, Kyle Lowry, Jason Kidd, David Robinson, LaMarcus Aldridge, Derrick Rose, Paul George, Kevin Garnett, Chris Paul and Marc Gasol in the Kindle Store. If you love basketball, check out my website at claytongeoffreys.com to join my exclusive list where I let you know about my latest books and give you lots of goodies.

Like what you read? Please leave a review!

I write because I love sharing the stories of influential people like Kobe Bryant with fantastic readers like you. My readers inspire me to write more so please do not hesitate to let me know what you thought by leaving a review! If you love books on life, basketball, or productivity, check out my website at claytongeoffreys.com to join my exclusive list where I let you know about my latest books. Aside from being the first to hear about my latest releases, you can also download a free copy of *33 Life Lessons: Success Principles, Career Advice & Habits of Successful People*. See you there!

Clayton

179

References

[i] Sumsky, Alex. "Kobe Bryant's Scouting Report is Worth the Read". *Basketball Forever*. 26 September 2016. Web

[ii] McCarney, Dan. "Quote History of Kobe". *NBA.com*. 11 April 2016. Web

[iii] Holmes, Baxter. "How Kobe Bryant Almost Became a Celtic". *ESPN*. 30 December 2015. Web

[iv] Youngmisuk, Ohm. "What if the New Jersey Nets had Drafted Kobe Bryant in 1996?". *ESPN*. 6 November 2015. Web

[v] Medina, Mark. "Kobe Bryant's 'Airball Game' in 1997 was a Defining Moment in His Career". *Daily News*. 15 January 2016. Web

[vi] "Round-the-Clock Purple and Gold". *Los Angeles Times*. 11 September 2009. Web

[vii] Yuscavage, Chris. "8 Things We Learned About Kobe Bryant From NBA TV's 'Kobe: The Interview'". *Complex*. 17 February 2015. Web

[viii] Turner, Broderick. "Kobe and Shaq: This Team Wasn't Big Enough for Both of Them, but it was Amazing While it Lasted". *LA Times*. 14 April 2016. Web

[ix] Broussard, Chris. "Wheels Come Off Laker Dynasty". *The New York Times*. 19 June 2004. Web

[x] Holmes, Baxter. "Where Kobe Bryant Found Inspiration for 62-Point Outburst 10 Years Ago". *ESPN*. 24 January 2016. Web

[xi] Stein, Marc. "Sorry, Wilt: You're no Kobe". *ESPN*. 24 January 2006. Web

[xii] DiChristopher, Toni. "Kobe Bryant Says He'd Rather Be Known for Venture Investing than Basketball". *CNBC*. 22 August 2016. Web

Made in the USA
Columbia, SC
22 May 2020